WOMEN WHO PIONEERED OKLAHOMA

Women Who Pioneered Oklahoma

Stories from the WPA Narratives

Edited by Terri M. Baker
and Connie Oliver Henshaw

Foreword by M. Susan Savage

UNIVERSITY OF OKLAHOMA PRESS : NORMAN

Library of Congress Cataloging-in-Publication Data

Women who pioneered Oklahoma / edited by Terri M. Baker and Connie
Oliver Henshaw.
   p. cm.
  Includes bibliographical references and index.
  ISBN 978-0-8061-3845-9 (hardcover : alk. paper) 1. Women
pioneers—Oklahoma—History. 2. Women pioneers—Oklahoma—
Correspondence. 3. Choctaw women—Oklahoma—History.
4. Minority women—Oklahoma—History. 5. Frontier and pioneer
life—Oklahoma. 6. Oklahoma—History. 7. Oklahoma—Social
conditions. I. Baker, Terri M., 1948– II. Henshaw, Connie Oliver, 1946–
  F699.W66 2007
  978.6—dc22

                     2007004542

The paper in this book meets the guidelines for permanence and dura-
bility of the Committee on Production Guidelines for Book Longevity
of the Council on Library Resources. ∞

We dedicate this book to the women who created Oklahoma through their experiences—terror, pain, sorrow, joy, and creativity—as they came to this area over the Trail of Tears, on later land runs, in wagons, on foot, in barges, and in trains. In the beginning, we researched them to satisfy our curiosity. Then as we read more interviews, we came to realize that a pioneer was someone who encountered changing conditions, and conditions changed for all women of the area as they participated in the beginning of what would become Oklahoma. In Indian Territory and then Oklahoma, women pioneered, creating life anew, and made a place where they could live together and prosper. The interviews with such women created moments of reinterpretation of the record that continue to inspire us. We are thankful for their courage and grit.

Contents

Illustrations

Foreword

Oklahoma's first one hundred years have been a time of growth and exploration for women, whose contributions to our state have only recently been chronicled and celebrated.

As a young girl growing up in Tulsa, I discovered one had to search to learn about the rich diversity of Oklahoma's women, their role in our state's history, their inner and physical strengths, their intelligence, resourcefulness, courage, and stamina.

I knew about my great-grandmother, who came to Oklahoma in a covered wagon and lived to see a man land on the moon. I knew that my grandmother was a woman in her early twenties before she was allowed the right to vote in our state, and who in 1992 was able to cast her vote for me when I was elected Tulsa's first woman mayor. The stories of these women were simply individual stories to me, part of our family's history, until I became a mother with two daughters.

As my own daughters grew, it became apparent that the individual family stories from generations of great-grandmothers, grandmothers, mothers, and aunts were cultural threads that connected my daughters to a legacy of strong women, influencing their values and contributing to their characters. The relationships among generations of strong women on both sides of their families created a tapestry of connections fundamental to shaping the focused, independent, and self-directed young women they have become.

Individual stories, such as those Terri M. Baker and Connie Oliver Henshaw have compiled, give us a picture of women in Oklahoma under different circumstances in different times whose very survival depended upon their individual strength. Their challenges seem daunting to us in this age of technology, easy transportation, and ready food. Yet in spite of the conveniences of our modern lifestyle, our roles are as pivotal to our families and communities as were those of these pioneering women. They remind us we share a legacy of strength, and their stories are both compelling and inspirational.

M. Susan Savage

Preface

This project began more than ten years ago when I (Terri Baker) started searching for interviews with Choctaw women in the Indian Pioneer Papers of Oklahoma because I was curious about my Choctaw ancestors. The collection grew and eventually included women of other races. Then, as a graduate student working with me, Connie Henshaw broadened the research and put the interviews together for a reader's theater production that was presented as part of the Annual Symposium on the American Indian at Northeastern State University. Theda Perdue saw it and suggested that we develop a book. A book! Two very busy women teaching what seemed like a zillion courses (by this time, Connie was a full-time instructor) looked at each other and said, "Let's do it."

A fascination for Oklahoma and an addictive curiosity about women who were our spiritual and biological grandmothers fueled our research for this book. During the process we found that when we would confide some discovered story to other women, they would immediately relate a story about their family, and a series of questions would begin. What did they wear, what were their houses like, how did they survive, how did they cook, what did they eat, did they work all the time, what games did they know, who did they marry and how did they meet their husbands, were any of them single or widowed, who helped them

during childbirth, and what was education like for them? Would
we have been so brave, so stalwart? Did the women think about
being strong or did they just do what had to be done? Conversations usually ended with quiet exclamations of "Wow!" When
we researched books on these early Western women, we quickly
discovered that the answers to such questions were not, for the
most part, found in the voices of the women from the nineteenth-
century Oklahoma frontier. We found some answers in photographs, but more answers in interviews. That is, the pictures showed
clothes, dwellings, and sometimes family members; however, we
found details in the interviews that indicated not only how women
managed their lives in the settings in the photographs, but also
how they felt about the everyday details of their lives—for example,
how they felt about the work involved, about special event clothes,
about the sounds of bugs in their walls, and about their fear of
snakes often found in their houses and yards.

This book takes its place among other works dealing with the
experiences of women in the American West. Fiction based on
the subject includes the *Little House on the Prairie* series written
by Laura Ingalls Wilder and *Let the Hurricane Roar* by her daughter
Rose Wilder Lane. Other fiction includes Willa Cather's *O Pioneers,*
for example. Autobiographies of American Indian women include
Sarah Winnemucca Hopkins's *Life Among the Piutes: Their Wrongs
and Claims* and the as-told-to autobiography *Pretty-Shield: Medicine Woman of the Crows* (originally published in 1932 as *Red Mother*).
The as-told-to autobiographies of American Indians as well as the
Western hero autobiographies of men share the characteristic of a
subject's relating his or her life experiences to a recorder-editor.[1]
This relationship of subject to recorder-editor underlies the Works
Progress Administration (WPA) interviews in the Oklahoma Indian
Pioneer Papers. The 1930s Works Progress Administration also
provided the material for the recently published *Women's Tales
from the New Mexico WPA* as it provided interviews for *The WPA
Oklahoma Slave Narratives.* The Oklahoma Indian Pioneer Papers
resulted when the University of Oklahoma teamed with the Oklahoma Historical Society (OHS) in order to secure a WPA project

grant. Grant Foreman acted as project director in Muskogee. Of
the two bound sets of original papers existing, one set is owned
by the University of Oklahoma, the other by the Oklahoma
Historical Society. While both sets are indexed, the index at the
OHS is more comprehensive. The Indian Pioneer Papers were
microfilmed and may be purchased from the OHS. The University of Oklahoma set is in microfiche. The John Vaughan Library
at Northeastern State University owns the OHS microfilmed collection, and we used this microfilm to research our project. The
volume and page numbers referenced here correspond to those
of the OHS microfilm.

Grant Foreman's project employed from eighty to one hundred fieldworkers throughout Oklahoma. The workers collected
eleven thousand interviews from people the fieldworkers believed
knew about pioneer life and had experiences that should be
recorded. The fieldworkers compiled the first drafts and sent the
papers to the project office, where they were edited to some
extent. The typed pages were bound into 112 volumes.

The fieldworkers were not experts; their names were taken
from relief rolls. They were primarily white, and, as an effort was
made to find workers with a sense of history and the skills to record
the interviews, they were generally well educated. The fieldworkers
were instructed to use the language of the person being interviewed
as nearly as possible.[2] The extent of the editing is unclear as is the
degree of mediation. The interviewers sometimes identify themselves as journalists and at other times as fieldworkers, leading us
to conclude that, although their skills varied, most were probably
journalists or local historians who possessed detailed knowledge
of the people in their geographical regions. Historical mistakes
sometimes appear, as these are recollections of elderly pioneers
rather than the writings of professional historians.

After a time we concluded that the best interviews were those
collected by women talking to other women. Sally McConnell-
Ginet suggests a reason for this: "The evidence shows that men
generally aim at individual conversational control, whereas women

aim at social conversational collaborations."[3] We believe that women interviewers simply invited the subjects to begin conversations and let them talk with only occasional prompts. The interviewers generally disappear from the narrative, allowing the subjects' voices to emerge unhindered. The subjects' commonality of experience, the as-told-to nature of the interviews, and the subjects' dominant voices led us to consider this work a collective autobiography. That is, while the details differ, the broad experience is common. Additionally, family stories relate memorable experiences, focus on dramatic details, exist within distinct historical periods, and are told many times, sometimes flowing from generation to generation, so that memory is working to mediate the life as in a memoir. These interviews share such characteristics. While we do not believe that our approach generalizes the individual experiences, we do believe that the evidence of commonality unifies them into a coherent story of pioneer women on the Oklahoma frontier.

In our research strategy we browsed specific volumes of the papers thoroughly, then, using clues provided in the interviews and in history books, we searched specifically for further interviews by using the index. In this way we managed to include a broad spectrum of interviews collected from women who lived through events that shaped the national culture and American identity. We changed the occasional punctuation mark or added a word here and there for the sake of clarity. Other than such minor changes, the interviews stand as recorded. Some interviews appear in third person, indicating the voice of a translator or an interviewer. Complying with Grant Foreman's agreement to maintain the anonymity of the interviewees, we do not provide their names or the names of their husbands. Further, we do not include entire interviews; rather we provide selections from the interviews and use ellipsis points to indicate portions that were cut from text.

The interviews show that women in this frontier culture had little opportunity to participate in the "woman's sphere" as described by Anne Firor Scott's 1971 book *The American Woman, Who Was She?*: "The most conservative view was that God had

created women to take care of men and children, and that whenever they took part in public activities they were being unladylike.
Women were seen as gentle, pious, sentimental, emotional—and
not very bright."[4] If fully embraced, these ideas about "true woman-
hood" would have made survival on the Oklahoma frontier difficult
if not impossible. Theda Perdue, Carolyn Johnston, and Glenda
Riley, as well as other scholars of the woman's experience, address
this issue too. The interviews also show that the women thought
their experiences were worth recording, a belief that comments
on the notion that women of the nineteenth century lacked confidence in the significance of their lives—a notion discussed in
1987 by Sidonie Smith in *A Poetics of Women's Autobiography*.[5]
While the interviews were not written autobiographies, the women
did believe in the importance of their lives. They reflected upon
their experiences during a nationally significant moment, and
knew that their words would be preserved for the future. If they
confronted the obstacle of confidence, they overcame it. They knew
their lives were significant.

One final argument for considering this a collective autobiography rests on the scholarship of James Olney, who states
that "autobiography is the literature that most immediately and
deeply engages our interest and holds it and that in the end seems
to mean the most to us because it brings an increased awareness,
through an understanding of another life in another time and place,
of the nature of our own selves and our share in the human condition."[6] We know that the questions women have posed to us about
these interviews are evidence of the subject's merit, of women's
sense of sharing a common humanity. We are not historians; rather
we are literary scholars with an interest in history. Therefore, the
chapter introductions are intended to provide historical context for
the interviews, which, as autobiography, are literature. A map and
photographs have been included to inform the reader of where
these women lived and by what elements they were surrounded as
they lived universal human experiences as women.

To begin in the spirit of these women, we offer this letter
exactly as it was written in 1841, in Eagletown, Indian Territory:

Oct 26 1841

My Dear husband

As you say I must write I must do so

I hope about this time you is on the road Lonny Folsom write to Robinson you is gone to Washington City I am very uneasy about you white people might kill you oh I Pray for you daily that you may come home safe your Heavenly Father will help you and will be with you all times

Since you say you are coming home children are so glad they look daily for you Peter dreams about you every night he just dance sing Papa is coming tell his sister Rhoda you must kiss Papa Lycurgus is got bad cough he is only one is got the cough some black children got too

Hoping cough is kill Graet many people in neighbourhood Sameul Byingtons Fathers wife and tow his children died last week and Capt hashabees tow grant children died one butterflys child is most dead also Capt Solomon all his children is sick Byington and his wife is not come yet from baggy willis Harkin has not pay me all money yet my children need flannel very much also no coffee and suger can be got in doakville no shoes for blacks I am you loving wife Rhoda Pitchlynn[7]

Acknowledgments

We wish to thank a number of people for their assistance. First, Theda Perdue helped more than we can say in encouraging us and making suggestions about research and publication. David La Vere read the manuscript and made very kind suggestions about historical events and references. At Northeastern State University, Phyllis Fife, Director of the Center for Tribal Studies, and Chris Malone, Director of the Living Literature Center, provided venues for discussion of our research. Delores Sumner, Special Collections Librarian at NSU's John Vaughan Library, and her staff helped us as we and our student workers researched. Paul Westbrook, Dean of the College of Liberal Arts at NSU, encouraged us, as did the staff of the College of Liberal Arts. We thank Janet Bahr, Interim Vice President of Academic Affairs, and Larry Williams, President of the university, for their support. Professor Bridget Cowlishaw in the Department of Languages and Literature read the introductions and made helpful suggestions. For technological assistance, we thank the staff of the NSU Microcomputing Services Center. Several students assisted us in checking and preparing citations and the bibliography and in finding specific interviews; they are Shanell Adams, Milena L. Robinson, Amanda Burnett, and Debra Smith. Undergraduate student office workers Kyle Meade and Grant Millikan performed various office tasks, and we thank them. The NDN Art Gallery in

Tahlequah, Oklahoma, assisted us in finding one of the photographs, and the staff of the Photographic Archives Division of the University of Oklahoma's Western History Collections kindly helped us to locate photographs as well. We thank the Bill Pittman family for allowing us to use the photograph of the Pittman couple outside the family dugout. Linda Henshaw served as typist for part of the manuscript. Heather Aziere and Shari Clevenger helped in checking final proofs. Peter Henshaw, Connie's son, helped us with photography. Connie thanks Ruby, Ruth, Judy, Betsy, Hooty, C. C., Lily, Aunt Loudie, Aunt Gladys, Aunt Marie, and "Miss Billie." Terri and Connie thank their friends and colleagues at NSU. Terri thanks her husband, Tom, and her son, Charlie, for their support. We thank R. D. Folsom for allowing us to use the letter from Rhoda Pitchlynn to her husband, Peter Pitchlynn, from whom R. D. Folsom is directly descended. We thank all of these people for patiently and good-humoredly helping us. Of course, any errors we acknowledge as our own.

WOMEN WHO PIONEERED OKLAHOMA

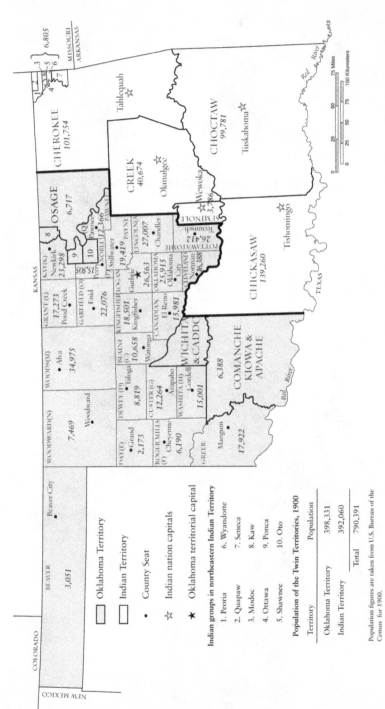

Oklahoma Territory and Indian Territory, 1900

Based on Charles Robert Goins and Danny Goble, Historical Atlas of Oklahoma, 4th ed. (Norman: University of Oklahoma Press, 2006), 145.

Indian groups in northeastern Indian Territory

1. Peoria   6. Wyandotte
2. Quapaw   7. Seneca
3. Modoc   8. Kaw
4. Ottawa   9. Ponca
5. Shawnee   10. Oto

Population of the Twin Territories, 1900

Territory	Population
Oklahoma Territory	398,331
Indian Territory	392,060
Total	790,391

Population figures are taken from U.S. Bureau of the Census for 1900.

Original county designations are in parentheses. During the early land openings in Oklahoma Territory, letters were used to designate counties until names could be officially adopted.

Legend:
☐ Oklahoma Territory
☐ Indian Territory
● County Seat
☆ Indian nation capitals
★ Oklahoma territorial capital

General History

In the southeastern Red River valley of Indian Territory in 1891, sixteen-year-old Lena married a man aged forty-five. The family says that her Choctaw parents accepted a traditional bride-price. For Lena, this bride-price was a wagonload of corn and two mules, paid by the white Texan who had come to Indian Territory in 1887 seeking marriage to an Indian wife who would bring him land rights. Lena's bride-price was high, a goodly sum indicating that the man could take care of her and protect her in a land afflicted by the violence that rapid change had brought.

In southwestern Oklahoma in the same decade, a wife in her early twenties, along with her two children under five years of age, accompanied her husband on a trip to Texas to visit his dying father. While attempting to ford the Red River just north of present-day Gainesville, her husband had a heart attack, and the horses foundered in quicksand. But the story had a happy ending. The young wife saved her husband's life, calmed and righted the horses, soothed her children, and, after regaining the Oklahoma bank of the river, continued with a guide on her journey. The couple celebrated their fiftieth wedding anniversary in 1937. This young mother and Lena never met. They were, however, sisters in spirit in a frontier land that offered little leeway to those weak in the will to survive.

Women had long resided in the area that is present-day Oklahoma, marrying, bearing and nurturing children, raising crops, weaving baskets, creating and ornamenting clothing, nursing the sick, burying the dead, cooking family meals and ceremonial feasts, and trading with neighbors. They lived in Oklahoma's disparate landscapes, all of which include elements of breathtaking beauty as well as terrible danger. They lived with the land as with a splendid and sometimes brutal mother. Then, beginning in 1828 and continuing for several decades, women traveled the Trail of Tears with their tribal communities as they suffered exile from their homes in the southeastern United States. These women traveling with their families ushered in a new era of pioneer women and set the stage for women and family groups who would follow when Indian Territory was open to non-Indian settlement later in the century.

First came the Choctaws from Mississippi, Louisiana, and western Alabama. Lena's great-grandmother would have been among those making the exodus on foot, in the few wagons provided, and on riverboats and barges. With family groups, women journeyed with the Creeks, Cherokees, Seminoles, and Chickasaws. Thousands of people died on the journey or shortly after arrival. The survivors settled in the eastern part of Indian Territory in the mountains and river valleys that merged with the plains to the west—home of the Indians who seemed wild to members of the federally removed "Five Civilized Tribes," so designated because of their early contact with whites and their assimilation of non-Indian customs.

In southeastern Oklahoma the soil offered fertility in its rich, black loam, a result of years of silt from rivers with mythical names—the Red and the Washita. From the 1830s through the early 1860s, the Choctaws and Chickasaws farmed cotton and corn in this soil, sometimes on large plantations tended by black slaves. North of Choctaw Nation, the Creeks and Seminoles worked the lush valleys of the Canadian rivers as the Cherokees tilled the earth surrounding the Arkansas, the Verdigris, and the Illinois rivers. In the mountains of eastern Indian Territory—the Ouachitas and the Ozark Plateau—farmers raised food crops in the valleys.

All the tribes tended cattle and hogs, which had been herded by their owners from their southern homelands, and wild game roamed the entire area. The Five Tribes worked immense corn and cotton fields, planted orchards, traded with neighbors, and secured goods from the stores at the market towns and the federal forts built to protect them from the western Indians—whose lands had been divided up without their full agreement and sometimes without their knowledge and then given by federal treaty to the removed tribes.

The Plains tribes invaded the lands occupied by the Five Tribes after Removal, primarily into Chickasaw land, which bordered immediately on Comanche and Kiowa areas. From Chickasaw ranches a constant flow of stolen horses moved into Comanche territory and down into Texas. Federal soldiers rode out after the thieves, but the raids continued. As Texas Indians fled the violence in their areas, Texas Rangers sometimes raided north into Indian Territory, for example, attacking "a Kotsoteka Comanche camp on the Canadian River."[1] In this beautiful land, human violence flared up much like the destructive wildfires that swept the grasslands and then were gone.

Still, the people farmed, hunted, created governments, held intertribal councils, and participated in both tribal and Christian religious ceremonies as they recovered from Removal and then blossomed in the years leading up to the white man's Civil War in the East.

In Indian Territory women and their families endured the horrors of this civil war in a terrifyingly personal way. This was not because great military forces clashed in nationally significant battles in Oklahoma, although battles did occur, resulting in catastrophic loss of life and wounds both physical and psychological. Equally devastating, the territory was left vulnerable as federal forces withdrew during the war years, the tribes split between Confederate and Union loyalties, and guerilla fighters rode in—from Kansas, Missouri, Arkansas, and Texas. Both guerillas and military units ranged up and down the eastern area of Indian Territory burning crops, looting food stores, carrying off anything of value, and randomly killing people and farm animals. In the wake of such turbulence, women, along with their children and their elderly, were left to survive as best they could in the plundered land.

During the Civil War, being left without their men, some women fled to Fort Gibson (Union) or Fort Washita (Confederate) seeking protection and food. Of the Five Tribes, only the Choctaws stood unanimously with the Confederates. Some Confederate families sought refuge in Texas. The Cherokees with Confederate sympathies near the borders of Kansas and Missouri moved south into lands controlled by Confederates. Some Cherokee family groups with Union ties traveled north to Kansas. A number of Creeks fled south to Choctaw Nation, others to the west. During the white man's Civil War, Indian Territory was often aflame as houses and outbuildings burned, destroying the means of survival and making vulnerable the lifeways that had been re-created after Removal. During the conflagration, nearly one-fourth of the population of the three tribes in the northern territory died, leaving many orphans and widows. Approximately nineteen thousand Indians sought refuge in settlements and forts at war's end.[2] This movement and displacement of people fell hard on women as they strove to feed their families and find their loved ones.

The end of the Civil War brought further problems to the women of Indian Territory as the price for participation in the war was set forth (the participation occurring without women's agreement). The price for participation was set in treaties between the federal government and various tribes. "As reparations, the government obtained land cessions and permission for railroads to cross Indian Territory. . . . Slavery was abolished and Freedmen were guaranteed property rights and certain aspects of citizenship among all but the Chickasaws." Token payments for ceded land were made to the tribes, and the railroads "foreshadowed the inevitable penetration of white culture." While the Chickasaw freedmen were no longer slaves, they possessed no land to farm within the Chickasaw Nation, much as the slaves in the South were free but possessed no land. "In the end, the Civil War proved more disastrous to the Five Civilized Tribes than to the Confederacy—for, despite the devastation and plunder of war, the southern states lost no land."[3]

Post–Civil War treaties opened the territory to railroads, which upset the tribal economic structure in the territory to the extent that entire towns simply disappeared as they were bypassed by the rails and their structures dismantled for construction on the new sites. Once thriving communities, Boggy Depot and Doaksville were two such places.

Once the land had been purchased by the railroad companies, white people began to arrive in ever-growing numbers, first to lay the rails and then to work in businesses along the track. The Choctaw-owned timber industry in the southeast supplied railroad ties for the track as well as the lumber for construction in the new railroad towns. Indian Territory's economy became increasingly integrated; many mixed marriages took place, disrupting traditional clan and town relationships; and populations moved about seeking opportunities in the changing economy.

American Indian women were once again stressed, their economic survival threatened both because of the death or maiming of so many of their men and because of the heightened competition for work, supplies, and services.

The tribes held their land in common, but, because so many Indian men were dead or maimed, and because many freedmen after the war possessed their own land or went to work for the railroads or the mining industry, farm labor was scarce. Tribes issued increasing numbers of permits to white workers who brought their families with them.[4] Many of these white tenant farmers were Civil War veterans and both owned and handled firearms with familiarity. Tribal members, also Civil War veterans, owned firearms, and after the war Indian Territory was occupied territory with tension among groups of people uncertain about customs, tribal sovereignty, and legal jurisdiction. Indeed, Glenn Shirley calls this new and drifting post–Civil War population "the refuse of humanity."[5]

As a growing number of non-Indians poured into Indian Territory, social structures changed rapidly. What before the war had been small, close-knit market, trading, and political communities surrounded by outlying farms, in the decades after the war began to include saloons, gambling halls, and workers connected to railroad construction. During the twenty-five years between 1865 and 1890, legal jurisdiction grew complex because the legal system was broken into specific tribal law enforcement agencies called

"Lighthorsemen" based within Indian Territory. The Lighthorsemen were answerable to tribal courts, and federal courts outside
the territory employed marshals who could ride into the territory
after those who broke white law.[6] In this twenty-five-year period,
non-Indians moving into the territory resulted in an influx of
strangers, many of them outlaws. Tribal newspapers advertised
recent shipments of silk and cotton stockings, wallpaper, flannel,
and coffee and enticed people to enter the market economy on all
levels. While traditional Indian citizens were content to produce
only enough for their families, progressive Indians eagerly sought
to modernize customs and civic structures and to participate fully
in the broader economy of the nation.

In the midst of this change, Indian Territory began to recover
from the devastation wrought by the Civil War. Women lived in and
among all of this complexity—the American Indians profoundly
connected to the land, the whites more casually connected, and the
blacks struggling for security and livelihood.

After the land openings, instances of theft, bootlegging, and
general violence abounded.

Most freedmen remained in Indian Territory after the war, and
by the time of statehood in 1907 they and their descendants, as well
as their former slaves, "outnumbered both Indians and first- and
second-generation Europeans in the Oklahoma population."[7]

As the years passed, the numbers of whites increased in the
territory and began to push for inclusion in the civic structures
available only to tribal citizens. The European American population desired access to public education and economic ventures.
They clamored to vote, lease land, and hold political office.
These non-Indian groups began to agitate for landownership.

People outside Indian Territory also hungered to own land,
and as the national population increased, landownership opportunities decreased. For those Americans on the borders of Indian
Territory, the lands beckoned. In the twenty years after the Civil
War, the population of the nation grew by almost 40 percent. By
1890 it had doubled. In the twenty years between 1870 and 1890,
the Texas population "grew from 818,579 to 2,235,527." In Kansas
the population "increased from 356,399 to 1,428,000."[8] Many of

these people then experienced the 1892–1893 drought in the Great Plains and suffered financial ruin.[9] In addition to native-born Americans, approximately two thousand European immigrants entered the Twin Territories every year for twenty years after 1890.[10]

White populations pushed to occupy Indian lands, and as this pressure to open the lands to white settlement increased, some Indians joined in but more resisted. In the late 1870s, the Boomers led by Captain David L. Payne organized, invaded Indian Territory in the area near what is today Stillwater, were removed by federal soldiers, explored throughout Oklahoma, and continued to agitate to open Indian Territory.[11]

Congress responded to the demands by breaking the treaties with Indians and opening Indian Territory to non-Indian settlement. The first land run took place on April 22, 1889, into nearly two million acres in the center of Oklahoma near present-day Guthrie.[12] Property staked out for ownership was composed of sections and parts of sections of land surveyed for the purpose. Of course, the most desirable parcels possessed water. Women of many races participated in the land runs, some with husbands, fathers, and brothers, and some individually. They rode on horses, in wagons and buggies, and some on the few trains that came in during the run, the trains proceeding by the rules at a horse's pace as people leapt off to stake claims.

After 1889, there followed the opening of the lands by run, allotment, lottery, and sealed bid until the last opening in 1906.

Some land was made available by allotment that divided the tribally owned property into parcels assigned to individual Indian owners. During this process, land was surveyed and a section (640 acres or one square mile) was divided into four parts so that generally an individual would be assigned one-eighth or one-quarter of a section. Other family members would also be allocated one-eighth or one-quarter. However, no provision was made to allot contiguous sections in the same area to members of the same family.

Tribal women were allotted land; however, full-bloods, both men and women, were declared incompetent by the government, and guardians were appointed.[13] Land and improvements left over after the allotment process were declared surplus and sold.

For more than a year after the first land run, there was little organized government, although town sites elected officials. During this period and for some time thereafter there was scant law in Oklahoma. The extent of violence associated with land openings is a matter of conjecture. On the one hand, interviews show that settlers who had staked out farmland went to work immediately making shelters and putting in crops. On the other hand, the town sites were booming frontier tent cities housing thousands of people in small areas and included saloons and gambling, and, naturally, every man carried a gun. "Sooners" who had entered the area illegally before the official opening were evicted.[14]

The Twin Territories of the land run era presented a human anthill that had been disturbed. The earth from which the anthill rose, however, nurtured all the people who had come seeking homes—the original American Indian groups, those early Removed Tribes who brought their customs from the South on the Trail of Tears, and the Civil War veterans and their families seeking peace and stability. Gamblers and even outlaws found refuge among the dense woods of eastern Oklahoma and the vast distances of the area's western plains. In beautiful and harsh Oklahoma, women jostled along with men for land and advancement. They made homes, bore children, died, farmed, and engaged in business. They built educational institutions and churches, and they developed cultural centers.

In doing so, in partnership with men, women created the state of Oklahoma.

ONE

Coming to Indian Territory and Early Oklahoma

Indian Removal forced the southeastern tribes of the United States to journey to Oklahoma. To cross the Mississippi from the Southeast people boarded steamboats, and, after the crossing, some traveled waterways to landings in Indian Territory. Many others walked, following military roads cut through the dense woods and mountains of eastern Oklahoma.

Indian Territory trails established over hundreds of years by American Indians evolved into cattle trails, roads, railroads, and eventually modern highways. State Highway 81 follows the original Chisholm Trail over which Texas cattle were herded north to Kansas. The early Osage Trace (later the Texas Road) running north and south is now four-lane U.S. Route 69. Along this highway run the tracks of the first railroad in Oklahoma, the Missouri-Kansas-Texas line, known as the Katy. The Katy tracks entered Oklahoma in 1870 from Kansas and crossed the Red River into Texas in 1872. In 1871 the Frisco line initiated the east-west rails in the state. This opening of Oklahoma to rail travel was a part of the post–Civil War agreements imposed on the Five Tribes for their participation in the Civil War.[1]

Railroads changed the economy, sped up communication with the outside world, and attracted and then supported a large non-Indian workforce. Businesses associated with railroads, such as lumbering, mining, and construction—as well as the land openings that began in 1889—also attracted significant numbers of non-Indians. Mixed in with these drifting populations were cowboys and tenant farmers, as well as outlaws, gamblers, and prostitutes.[2] And this mixed population added to the lawlessness of the area. The railroads spurred on the cattle industry because most of the cattle drives ended at railheads where the cattle could be sold and organized for shipment out of the territory, leaving the drovers free to celebrate in the saloons amid the rowdier elements of the railroad towns. The cattle industry grew rapidly, and the novelty of trains invited people to gather in the towns to watch them roll in.

Lena's story exemplifies this pattern of changing transportation and its effects. Lena, a Choctaw, and her "white Indian" husband produced one son. Lena's son married the daughter of a man who wandered into Indian Territory and followed the gambling trail in the northeastern part of the territory with his Cherokee wife after the Civil War. The gambler, his Cherokee wife, and their children traveled the Texas Road south, where they became tenant farmers on the ranch owned by Lena and her husband. There the gambler–tenant farmer's daughter met and married Lena's son near Caddo, a town along the old Texas Road and the site of a railhead along the Katy. Such was the diversity of the experiences of travel to and within Indian Territory and early Oklahoma that people entered the area from all points of the compass in all manner of transport following all sorts of routes.

The interviews document that women traveled to get to Indian Territory and also traveled a good deal inside the general area, for the most part with men but sometimes alone or with their children, to find relatives or to get supplies. They frequently met with harsh conditions. Journeys of several weeks were sometimes required, and often travelers were beset by thunderstorms, floods, and high winds. Voyagers crossed rushing rivers, were endangered by stampedes, and camped in pouring rain. Of course, food was often scarce and emerged as a central theme on these excursions—travelers encountered wild game on the way; carried provisions such as poultry and flour; found native fruits ripe along the trails and hauled their cooking equipment along.

In the interviews the women did not speak of courage, apparently considering what we might label remarkable bravery to be simply the norm for getting around on the frontier.

Anglo from Texas, b. 1867

The rhythmic pounding of horses feet and the swishing of knee-high sage grass against the wagon were hardly audible above the bawling and bellowing of a herd of frightened, frenzied cattle which were surrounding and following the little caravan headed west through the old Wagoner Pasture of Oklahoma.

I sat in the wagon holding the reins, and beside me, pressed close to my side, was my little son, two years old. I was afraid we could be crushed and stomped by a wild stampede of cattle. Any way one looked there was a vast expanse of grass, miles and miles of it, melting away into the horizon, and there were herds of cattle as far as the eye could see.

Presently my husband wound his way among the cattle and rode up to the side of the wagon. He assured me that there was no danger from the cattle, and that no harm would befall me and I felt less fearful.

In the wagon were our household goods, behind came our cattle and horses which comprised all our worldly possessions.

We were headed for the plains of Texas, but we never reached them. This was in 1891, and we came west after a short stay in the eastern part of Oklahoma. Formerly we had lived in Dallas County, Texas. (31:159–60)

Anglo from Tennessee, b. none given

I arrived [in Muskogee, Indian Territory] on the evening of September 8, 1892. When the train pulled into the station, I noticed that the platform was swarming with people and I wondered what the attraction was. Later, I found out that the folks just went down to see the train come in. The one reporter from the one newspaper in town was there to take note of who stopped over or passed through. The next morning I looked out and the streets were perfect rivers, a terrible rain-storm having occurred in the night.

. . .

United States Court had been established in Muskogee not long before [1892] and the town was full of ambitious young lawyers and other young men who had been attracted to the new country. Among them was Mr. Clifford L. J[—] whom I afterward married; Mr. Wayman Crow Jackson; and Mr. N. A. Gibson, whom I had known in Tennessee. In fact I was, perhaps, in a way responsible for Mr. Gibson's coming to the Territory. He came to see us in our home in Brownsville, Tennessee, and said he would like to make a change and I suggested that he go to the Indian Territory. I gave him letters of introduction to Mr. C. L. J[—] and Mr. W. C. Jackson and he came west. On being pleased with the outlook for a young lawyer, he decided to locate in Muskogee. In the following April, he returned to Memphis and married his sweetheart, Miss Florence Davidson, and they immediately came to Muskogee. Mr. Gibson is now one of the most prominent attorneys in Oklahoma, located in Tulsa. (31:14, 16)

Anglo, b. none given

When we lived there at Bower, we were on the road from Eufaula to McAlester; one branch of the road also went east toward Quinton, Enterprise and Fort Smith. In those days there were no bridges in the Territory; you crossed the creeks and rivers at a ford or on a ferry. The Canadian River got up fast in those days. I remember once when we went to Eufaula that the river was low enough to ford, then, before we came back it was so high that we couldn't cross on a ferry. There was a ferry where the North and South Canadian Rivers ran together; it was called Brassfield's Ferry. There were other ferries at places all over the Indian Territory where traffic was thick enough to make them necessary and where the water was too deep to be forded easily.

In 1905 we moved to Newberg, close to where Atwood is now; the Missouri Oklahoma & Gulf Railroad was just coming through there. We lived in that community until after statehood. (89:30–31)

Anglo from Tennessee, b. 1-8-1870

My parents were married in England at a young age. Soon after this they sailed to America and settled in 1867 in Tennessee, where I was born January 18, 1870. When I was small, they moved to Texas where my father died.

I came with my mother to the Indian Territory in 1888 when I was eighteen years old.[1] We came by wagon and team; this was in the days of riding skirts and side-saddles. I had a pony all of my own and this I rode most of the way from Texas. We crossed Red River near Gainesville on an old ferry boat known as Bounds ferry. After much persuasion my pony and I, with the wagon, went aboard the old ferry boat. The boat got stuck on the sand long before it banked and I rode my pony off into the river and came on out, then as we journeyed along in the Territory, which was almost a no-man's-land, I got the thrill of my life in this way. There was only one road and of course, we were traveling over it. Drinking water was very scarce and as we were traveling along badly in need of water, I spied a spring some ways off the road and taking a jug from the wagon, I rode up to the spring, intending to return at once with water for the rest of the family, as they were driving on. I reached the spring and a man and woman were there. I got to talking to them and stayed longer than I intended and when I rode back to the road, I saw the wagon had gotten out of sight. I started pursuit and had gone only a short ways when all at once I came face to face with two Indians, the first I had ever seen. Well, I couldn't go back so I began lashing my pony with my riding quirt and I guess I would have run down those Indians had they not cleared the road. Anyway, after some two miles of hard racing, I caught up with the wagon and thereafter I kept in close contact with it as we traveled on. We were seven weeks on the road and finally stopped and settled at Chink, some few miles from where Ardmore now is. (89:34–36)

Anglo from Texas, b. 1-9-1877

You had as much land as you could fence around and care for up here. No one seemed to know who really owned it. There was no one to pay taxes to. The United States claimed it twice and Texas claimed it twice while my people occupied the land. We were two miles from Red River near the place where Boggy Creek runs into the Red River.

Years went by and the family was really a large clan with some of them living in Texas and some up here, and one was for all and all for one with whatever was needed. Mother and Father were married and I was born and other children were born. I was never very strong and the doctors thought that if I were brought farther north and allowed a wilder, freer life I possibly would get stronger. We made many trips back and forth always either in a covered wagon or on horseback. We encountered high waters and other dangers often.

I remember once we had to wait on the banks of Red River several days before we could cross as the water was so high we could not even be ferried across. There were quite a few people gathered on the banks of the river waiting. When it had run down enough to deem crossing safe, people began to drive their teams on the ferry boat and unhitch them from the wagons. All the people on the boat stood up and by the time we were in mid-stream, it was clearly noticeable that the boat was overloaded and was slowly sinking. You know, animals are very quick to sense danger and the horses became very restless. Father took all the harness off his horses leaving them free. He knew his horses were good swimmers and believed they would save themselves if they were free to do so. Grandmother was with us. Father came and stood near me and said to me, "Now if I get ready to jump, you cling to my coat and never turn loose for anything." Grandmother could swim too so we hoped to stand free. Not a person was making a sound except a few who had dropped to their knees and were praying. Some way we got across but the water in the boat was up to my waist when the boat touched the other bank. (89:61–63)

. . .

There was no place to go but Mother was always very strict about having us rest on Sunday. One Thursday Father came in to Mother and said, "The millet and oats are ready to cut and I simply must go to Chillicothe before I start cutting them. One day to go, one day to stay, and one day to come home will throw it on Sunday, but I simply must go." The team was gotten ready—we never started off for a trip without sheets and bows on the wagon and Father said that Sister and I could go with him. We trotted over and got there all right that night. We stayed in the wagon yard and as we were getting ready for bed, Father called to us, "Girls, you must arise early in the morning and get through your shopping for there is lightning in the southwest and you never know what the river will do when it rains—we must get started back."

The next morning it was raining but not hard. We got our errands done speedily and started for home, but when we got to the river, she was bank full. One of our uncles lived on the south bank of Red River. We turned and went to his house. We left home on the last day of May. This was now the first day of June. Every day we went to try and cross, but it was the fifteenth of June before we ever got home.

There was a small band of Indians who had been down to Wichita Falls waiting to cross. They had no provisions with them so were nearly starved. The day we did cross it took the Indians and all the cowboys on horses all day trying to settle the sand so we could cross. There was a bunch of people waiting to cross. When we got home after fifteen days, Mother had eaten everything like sugar, coffee, etc., up and was out of coal oil. She had taken lard and made a grease lamp in case any of them got sick in the night. She and the rest of the family did not get up until day light and went to bed at dark. (89:61–63, 72–73)

Anglo from Tennessee, b. 1890

It was the prettiest sight I ever saw. All that tall grass waving and the trees and flowers. We were thrilled ecstatic. We had to camp out one night, then we children got scared. We just expected the Indians to come and scalp us any minute. We could hear the owls hooting and the frogs hollering, but after a while when nothing had happened, we got over our fright and sat around the fire and roasted peanuts until late bedtime. We were too excited to think of going to sleep for a long time. But in the day time we had the most fun riding in the log wagon drawn by oxen. I cannot recall the name of the other family. (89:98)

Anglo from Texas, b. 1881

There were twelve children in my father's family of whom I was the oldest. Grandfather Jenkins, my mother's father made his home with us and sometimes members of my mother's family stayed with us, so there was a goodly family of us all indeed. All during my early childhood there was always talk of going to Greer County for free land for a homestead. Our home was sold in McLennan County [Texas] and we started. Father would come to some ranch man who wanted land cared for or a lot of work done; we would rent for a year or more and stay but always our yearning hearts wanted a lot of land and a home of our own.

In the early '90's Father came to Greer County but found so much confusion about titles that he decided to wait until he would know whether Texas or the Federal Government owned Greer County.[2]

We stayed in Jack County several years and we never seemed to have enough water for the family or the stock. When the case was settled in 1896, Father came up to Greer County to buy a claim or to file on land. When he left the last words my mother said were, "Be sure and get a place with a lot of good water." Father could find no place in Greer County with good water as most places there had no water at all. He started home by way of Indian Territory but in and around Duncan he found plenty of good water and land to rent. It was a wooded country and Father thought that Mother would like that so he rented it and came on home to gather the crop and sell out all the things that he could and move to the Indian Territory.

We were a little leary [sic] of the Indians but Father rented from a white man and he told us he did not think there were many Indians that far south which proved to be true. I think it was

December of the year for I remember the year was nearly gone when we got started. We had two covered wagons but not much household goods—mostly bedding and clothing in these wagons. We drove horses. We had a coop full of chickens tied on to one side of a wagon and an old white cow on a lead rope behind one wagon. We have everything to camp with, a skillet, a bucket to make coffee in and a Dutch oven to bake bread. We had one tent that was put up every night and all who could not sleep under the tent slept in the wagon.

We were about a week making the trip. (89:110–12)

Anglo from Texas, b. 1872

Now in 1899 our family and four other families started from Archer County, Texas, in five covered wagons with a hundred and fifty head of cattle and some horses. When we got to Archer City there were fifty more covered wagons on their way to Oklahoma Territory.[3] I remember one night we got all of the cattle bedded down and we ourselves went to bed. We woke up early next morning and every one of the cattle were gone. My husband went back four or five miles hunting for them. Finding no trace of them, he came back and went down the road that we were to go on and found them down the road about two miles and they had all bedded down again.

We crossed Red River at Doan's Crossing. There was straw in the river bed and a man to pilot us across, but we were held up at the river three days for our cattle to be inspected for ticks. When we came across one county, we hadn't been able to get water for our stock and we saw a house back in a pasture with a windmill. My brother said, "Here is where I am going to water these cattle." And when they got to the windmill, out came a man with his shotgun and said that we couldn't stop for he had lost two hundred head of cattle. My brother grabbed his gun and said that the cattle were going to drink and that he would pay for every tick that he got off of our cattle.[4]

There were four families stopped in Greer County, so we were the only ones that came on to Roger Mills. We were on the road six weeks and camped out and cooked on camp fires. Wood was scarce so we had to cook with cow chips most of the time. We had a tent but the rest of the crowd had to sleep on the ground or in the wagons. I guess there were about thirty boys along, acting cowboys.

We first stopped at Berlin and rented a dugout from a Doctor Morrison.[5] We paid him $10 for a month's rent and we got there just the night before that awful prairie fire broke out that burned up the Perry family. They were living in tents and had plowed no fireguards. We stayed in the dugout two weeks then filed on a claim over on Beaver Creek twelve miles northeast of Elk City. On the claim we lived in our tent until we could get a dugout made. And then we learned that another man had filed on the claim so we gave it up and filed again and dug another dugout and the same thing happened again. So we filed three times before we got a home. We made a third dugout and covered it with boards and when it rained it just poured in and I would set buckets, pans and tubs all over the beds trying to keep them dry. (89:133–35)

Anglo, b. 6-14-1886 Jefferson County, Missouri

I was six years of age when my parents came to Oklahoma February, 1892. My father came before we did, coming on a freight car, with our household supplies; he also brought some stock. Mother and the rest of the family came down on the train. My father made the Cheyenne and Arapaho run on horseback starting from the section line, a mile south of El Reno, and locating a claim four miles south and six miles west of El Reno. (89:159)

Anglo from Texas, b. 2-21-1868

My father's name was M. D. Hensley and my mother's maiden name was Myra A. Byrd. Both were born in North Carolina. We lived in Wise County, Texas, when we decided to move to Oklahoma.

We were all very poor, and I think that was the deciding factor in our coming to Oklahoma. It was a land of opportunity. There were some four families of us: my father's family; two brothers and their families; and my husband and I. Of the thirteen in my father's family, twelve are still living. I have eight children, all living. G. C. Hensley, one of my brothers, became the first sheriff of Jackson County.

We came through in thirteen covered wagons and a hack. I suppose we had the usual experiences of the pioneer on this trip. There were no bridges and it was necessary to ford all rivers and creeks. (12:537)

Anglo from Iowa, b. 4-5-1872, parents from Indiana

My husband and I were married in Gaines County, West Texas, and soon after our marriage decided to come to the Indian Territory, so that fall, 1891, we packed our belongings in a covered wagon and started on our way.

We forded Red River, into the Indian Territory, northeast of Quanah, Texas.

We hit a little strip of country just inside the Territory that had "gyppy" water but we were prepared for that, as we had a big water keg in our wagon which we carried full of water for such emergencies.[6]

We did our cooking over an open fire in Dutch ovens. We had two large ovens about fourteen inches in diameter and they were about five inches deep. They had three legs about two inches long, and a big heavy cast iron lid that had a raised rim about an inch high around the outside of the lid. The rim around the lid was what held the coals of fire on top, like a stove oven. I made sour dough biscuits, on our trip, because of not having milk to make ordinary biscuits. Sour dough biscuits are good and when they raise like they should, they resemble rolls.

We carried a supply of flour, bacon, and potatoes on our trip but most of the time we had fresh meat. My husband had a shot gun and he killed wild turkeys, quail, prairie chickens and rabbits, one or the other, every day.

We traveled a road that led on to the south side of the Wichita Mountains, and was in sight of Quanah Parker's home, which looked very nice from where we were.[7] (12:462–63)

Anglo from Arkansas, b. 1877

My father and mother came with a wagon train. My father and Mr. John Goodrich led this wagon train. That was 1882. We crossed the Canadian River at Johnsonville, Indian Territory on the government trail; this wagon train separated at Whitebead, Indian Territory. My father settled there. I was very young at the time I don't know where the rest of the people went. My father went to hauling freight from Caddo to Fort Sill; there were lots of turkey, pecans, grapes and plenty of fish in the Washita River.[8]

My father S. B. Stark built us a one room log house at Whitebead; there was not very many houses there then. James Rennie owned a store there.

This country was wild then, I have seen the Indians pass our house on ponies with their faces painted.

When we were coming from Arkansas to Whitebead, Indian Territory, I was riding with my father and mother and three brothers in the front wagon. After we had traveled for several days, my father said, "We are in the Indian Territory," late that evening a big group of Indians, on horses, stopped our wagon train. One of them did the talking; he talked to my father and Mr. Goodrich. He wanted to trade, he said. My father asked him what he wanted to trade for, the Indian said, "Trade Squaws" Father said, "No." Then the Indian said, "Papoose." Father said, "No." The Indian then shook his head and rode away and the rest of the Indians followed him, whooping and hollering. Some of them (I can remember) had their faces painted and lots of feathers in their hair, or fastened on their heads some way. We were never bothered any more. (12:509B–510)

Creek, b. 1864

I was born at Boggy Depot, in 1864. My mother, Kizzie Lewis, was a full-blood Creek Indian and my father, William Shaw, a white man. He was a native of Maryland and came to Indian Territory before the Civil War. I was their only child.

As many of the Indians did, my parents immigrated to Texas to escape the ravages of war. At the close of the war they returned to the Choctaw Nation and lived for a time at Boggy Depot, where I was born. (12:138)

Anglo from Texas, b. 1891

I was born in Texas, about ten miles north of Weatherford. The log house sat near a running stream named Clear Fork. All the buildings in the yard were made of logs. There were three buildings in the yard that we used all the time. None of them had any windows. The big house was where we lived and slept. About ten yards away from this was a smaller one where we cooked and ate and a little further on was still another house we called a smokehouse, where all of our food was kept except what was used every day in the kitchen. All of these houses were chinked and daubed with lime and mud between the logs. My father went to the woods and cut the logs and built the houses the last year of the Civil War.

I grew up and married on this place. There was not a mortgage or delinquent taxes on it for more than fifty years, while it belonged to Mother and Father.

In 1891, my husband and I left Texas and started to the Chickasaw Nation. We had three little girls. We started out in a covered wagon, driving two little mules. It was November. About one month before we started I was bitten by a centipede and the poison had never gotten out of my system and I could not walk upright when we left for the purpose of finding a new home.

Our first stop was at Ardmore. There was a blacksmith shop, a wagon yard, two stores, and a few homes which made up the town. The hogs were bedded in the streets until you could hardly get through. We wandered around about a month and a half in that country trying to find land to buy or rent. Finally we camped about eighteen miles north of Ardmore between two streams. The larger of the streams was called Boggy. This was a good camping ground and there were several families camped in the valley between the streams. While we camped there my husband and another man found a wild turkey roost and we had a lot of turkeys to eat. We had deer while we camped there. Here we heard of land we might rent. There was a log home just put up made from green logs and no windows in it but we were so glad to get land to cultivate and a house to live in; we rented and stayed two years. The house was 20 feet long and at least half as wide. After two years we moved a little farther north and went to another log house. This house had a good board roof on it and a little brush arbor out in front to be used to sit under in the summer. We raised cotton and corn. We had lots of vegetables to eat but did not enjoy them so much for we were always sick; it was such an unhealthy country. There were no schools near enough for my children to attend.

There were wild grapes, plums, persimmons, and plenty of pecans. You go out any time and kill all the squirrels you could eat. Our post office was called Hewitt. I think it is called New Wilson now and is in an oil field.

After staying on this place five years we started west to what was then Oklahoma Territory. We now had five children, the baby only one month old. It was February and the day we started was as pretty a day as one would want to commence a journey. We found an old house to camp in when night came but during the night it began to rain. It rained for two days and one night and late in the afternoon of the second day, some people came along and told us to move along. Still it rained, but the next morning we loaded up and started on our way. We traveled all day in the rain. We stopped to camp at a little store house in a clearing called James. We stopped under a big tree and just as we stopped our team, a squirrel ran up the trunk of the tree and my husband killed it. We had squirrel for supper. After supper we propped the wagon tongue up with the breast yoke and spread some quilts over it and let them hang down on the sides. My husband and the oldest children slept under that. It rained all night and in the morning the ground was so soft as we went along the hubs of the wagon would sometimes drag in the mud. We got stuck several times but somebody would come along and hitch on and pull us out and we would go on. Here we stayed a week at Comanche Town until it began to fair up. When it had faired up a little, we started on again, but the road was so soft that we would stick every little while and would have to be pulled out.

At last we got to what was called Snyder Flats and here we stuck and stuck, I don't know how many times, before we got to the town. That was the little town that has blown away so many times. It was new then and the houses were made of tin. There were some tents. We found a little house to camp in. The next morning we drove on west and got to Otter Creek and camped. In the night it began to rain again. They were putting the railroad through to Kldorado [perhaps Colorado or Eldorado] and there were several campers. They had some women with them and when it began to rain, some of the women came over to where we were camping and insisted that the children and I come over to the tents and sleep. The three little ones and I slept in the tent with them and my husband and the two oldest children slept in the wagon. The next morning it was still raining. We cooked breakfast and ate with them. They invited us to stay that day which we did, and the night also. During the night the two Otter Creeks came together and the water was running through the tents, so we left there without any breakfast. They had the railroad track built so the work train could cross over and we walked out on the rails. We had to track back the way we came. A family not far from the creek took us in and kept us a week. There was a little mound that the horses could stand on and my husband walked back and forth on the railroad and kept them fed. We got the man who ran the work-train to bring our bedding out. One of the men who was camped with us said he was an old cowhand and had been in this country a long time. He said campers were always getting caught in there and he and a lot of cowboys had tied their ropes to the tree tops a lot of time, and loaded women and children on tops of tables or any flat surface and could row them out by pulling the ropes. He said two old stubborn men would not come out and leave their things, and he swam out twice a day to take them food. The man were staying with said he intended to be a cowman but did not get on the trail but once. They came to a big river and it was up and they could not get the cattle to go into it. So he pushed one old bull off into the water and jumping off his horse, he grabbed the old bull by the tail and by slapping him with his hat and yelling, he kept him going the right way across and the other cows all followed. And that was enough for him.

After unloading so many of our things the team could pull out. We left Otter Creek and made it safe to North Fork of Red River. It was still misting and the river was up. We were afraid to drive into the water. There was a man plowing near the river and we tried to hire him to pull us across. We told him he could hitch his team in front of ours and pilot us across. He told us there was no use in that as the river was perfectly safe for us to just drive in. So we started across and we would have made it all right had not one of our mares been afraid of quick sand. About middle way she laid down and would not get up until she was unhitched from the wagon. My husband took the other mare and by making a lot of trips he got us all out and a lot of the things too.

It took some time to get five children and me out and by that time, some cowboys came along and tied their lariat ropes on the end of the tongue of the wagon and pulled the wagon out.

We got out and traveled a little farther and got to a little town. I have forgotten the name of it but we stopped to camp for my husband was wet to his waist and by now the rain was snow and we were all cold. The next day brought us to where Altus is now. Here we got acquainted with a man who lived farther west across Salt Fork. He had killed some kind of wild cat and had stuffed its hide and nailed it to a plank. It was as big as a good size dog and had black and yellow spots. I did not think much about the stuffed hide then as I knew we had another river to cross that evening. So we followed the man out of town and when we got to the river, the man hitched his team in front of ours and we crossed safely. We went on to his house and spent the night with him. He just lived in a little dugout and cooked on a fireplace. Their beds were one legged bunks. The railings of the beds were logs just stuck in the walls of the dugout. The next day we drove into Duke. We had to go through the pastures as the roads were so soft we did not dare go over them for fear of being stuck again. So you see through all this travel we had been out but one night. The people were good to us and took us in and it never cost us a penny except at the wagon yard.

We got land and began to farm and are still farming. We used to make good crops. We made eleven bales of cotton the first year and I cannot tell you how much maize and cane we made. There were lots of wild plums on that first place. I made a plum pie the sixth day of June and we still had plums on the trees in September. I cannot tell you how many plums were sold off of the place.

The next year we moved over on the Salt Fork. It was a dry year but that did not keep the river from coming down and overflowing. I watched the river come down and cut out seven acres of our corn that was planted next to the river, and carry it on down the river, land and all. I crossed the river to Mangum when the water was over the bridge. I stayed here five years and made pretty good crops, considering the water and dry hot winds.

I have spent some years in New Mexico and proved up a claim out there but that is not much of a cotton country. I have stayed here most of my life; after my husband died as my eldest children were girls I thought I had to stay in a cotton country so they could help make the living. What little schooling they got they had to go three and four miles to get it and a lot of times they had to drive the old gray mare. I have washed and ironed for sixty-five cents a dozen to help with the expenses when we had a dry year. (31:52–61)

Anglo, b. 4-3-1870 Osage County, Missouri

In 1887 I was married to James Thomas J[—] who was born in Georgia December 27, 1855.

My father and some of my other relatives had moved to the Chickasaw Nation in the meantime and they thought the new country was a good place for young folks to get a start in life, so in 1889 my husband and I moved to the Chickasaw Nation and rented some land near a little place called Elk not far from the Arbuckle Mountains; the nearest stream was called Eight Mile Creek because it ran eight miles before it emptied into Wild Horse Creek.

We had a covered wagon and a team of ponies and every thing we had was in the wagon except a milk cow.

Our brother-in-law and his family moved with us; they also had a covered wagon and a team of ponies, and everything they had also was in the wagon, except a cow. Our brother-in-law's name was J. C. Wolf but he was not my kin; he only had the same name as my maiden name. We wanted to bring our cows along so my husband and J. C. took turns at walking and driving the milk cows behind the wagons and when we women would get tired of riding in the wagons, which made very slow progress, we would walk and drive the cows and let the men drive the wagons and mind the babies. We were two weeks making the trip.

. . .

My father recovered and we came back to the Territory but later went to Georgia and lived three years. We were not satisfied in the Old State so we came back to Oklahoma and when the Kiowa Country opened in 1901, we bought a farm of one hundred and one acres.[9]

We paid six hundred dollars for it and lived awhile in a half dugout and later my husband built a three room house and we improved the place.

We sold that farm and have since owned two other farms in Kiowa County.

Our family has grown up here and I have had many experiences in the new country. We now live in Lone Wolf and will celebrate our fiftieth wedding anniversary next November, 1937. (31:271, 275)

Anglo, b. 10-16-1856 Indianapolis, Indiana

It was in the winter time, about January, I believe 1884, when Barney decided to move from Atoka to Doaksville. It took us four days to make the trip. We had good teams and wagons, and we were young, and did not mind the hardships. In fact, they were adventures to us. We camped one night at an old Indian meeting house; I never learned the name of that place. The house was locked up, but a shed had been blown down and it made a shelter, under which we camped out of the snow. The next night we built up a log heap, burned it and warmed the ground, spread grass on that, then our beds on top, pulled our wagons up on either side, with a wagon sheet across from one wagon to the other and across the back, making a shelter from the snow and kept a log heap burning all night out in front. The next night we went over the hills to old Spencer Academy. There was no school there then; I imagine the school had been abandoned. We camped in the old school building that night, and were comfortable. I will never forget how beautiful the trees were laden with snow. The limbs of the trees overlapped the road. The horses could travel only a few miles each day. It looked like the snow was a foot deep.

The fourth night we were nearly to Doaksville, and we stayed with friends about four miles from Doaksville. Then the next day we went on to the old fort place which we had rented. (38:120–21)

Anglo from Kentucky, b. 11-8-1867

Before August 1901, a trip was made by my husband bringing over one hundred head of cattle from Olney, Texas. My husband came back for me. We drove through in a covered wagon. When we crossed Red River we had to drive in the bed of the river as there were no bridges. Luckily the river was very low, so we had no trouble crossing.

As our daughter stayed in Fort Worth, attending school there, I felt very lonesome in this new country. Onward we drove to our new location where our cattle were. Soon my husband pointed saying, "There is your new home." All I could see was a big tree and a tent beside it. I really felt discouraged; then I thought that wasn't any spirit to start with in a new home. (37:266)

Creek from Indian Territory, b. 1859

Most of our relations were living near Hickory Ground and Eufaula and had proved their rights and were enrolled as Creek Indians.[10] My mother's father was a Creek but her mother and her husband were white. Mother was born in Texas and lived there until her people persuaded her to bring us up here and get our land as they were doing.

. . . We were met by a rig and were taken out to my aunt's home near Bun Ryal Crossing. . . . We children kept trying to go to sleep but the rocks were as large as elephants and every time we would doze off to sleep, the buggy would hit a big rock and wake us up. Mother kept looking for a public road such as she had been used to in Texas. We were on a horse trail that had been made by Indians and cowboys who were riding horseback and no vehicles were supposed to travel over it. We passed that way many times though while we lived out there. (94:257–58)

Cherokee, and Creek or Seminole, b. 1894

Father drove oxen to haul logs. The wagon axle was bigger than a water bucket; the tires of the wheels were about eight inches wide. The yoke was of wood but it had a steel bolt holding it together, or that might have been to fasten them to the wagon. I really don't know which.

He was coming from work, hauling logs for a rail fence for himself. A bad looking cloud was coming fast and he ran into the house, not thinking to loosen the oxen. They went under a black-jack tree about a half mile from the house. When the storm was over and he went to see about the oxen, they had been hit and killed by lightning. (37:193, 197)

Cherokee, b. 1864

My father was driving four oxen to an ox wagon. Their traveling was slow, but not so bad as was the traveling of those who had first come this way many years before as now there were roads, not good ones, but they were roads, fords, and more bridges.

When we reached Kentucky, my grandmother who was with our family, became too ill to travel farther, so Father was compelled to stop there with his family, letting his friends come on without him.

We lived here till I was ten years old. During this time, my grandmother died and the thing I remember best about her are the big aprons that she used to wear. While we lived in Kentucky, Father worked at the tanning trade. Hearing of the new home occasionally and knowing that his father was in it and that he had some half-brothers here in Indian Territory, he decided to come to them. . . .

So this time, my parents started in an ox wagon drawn by four oxen and a buggy drawn by a horse. There were father, mother, us eight children, Eliza, John, Mollie, David, Mattie, Sarah Ann, Jimmie and myself, Emma Virginia Lee.

We were four weeks on the road from Kentucky and would stop on the road and rest and do our washings in the streams that we crossed. We stopped at Neosho, Missouri, and from there after Father made some inquiries about his half-brothers, we came on to Muskrat's Mill where Father left the family and went to find his brothers.

He found them near Tahlequah and when he had found them, of course, they did not know him, but they had heard their father say that he had left a small son back in Tennessee, so one of them asked my father, who was my grandfather, and they, knowing him by that name, were satisfied, and wanted him to locate near them, so Father rented a small place two miles from Mayesville. So Father came back to us and after four weeks at Muskrat's Mill, moved his family to this place. (21:246–48)

Anglo from Texas, b. 1869

When I was eight years of age, my parents came from Stevens County, Texas, to the Indian Territory and settled near a place called Jimtown, and for years my father went to Gainesville, Texas, for our supplies. He would make the trip with oxen twice a year, in the spring and fall, and would be away from home two weeks each time.

There were ten children of us and he would buy our shoes and clothing and groceries that would keep such as lye to make soap, lamp wicks, tea, flour, soda, baking powder, and some simple home remedies in case of sickness. Later, we could get supplies at Chickasha at the Indian Agency if it was really necessary.[11] (100:405)

Anglo from Texas, b. 1857

We did not have very good health where we lived and land was so high that we could not get any more. My husband went

prospecting for a country where he could get more land and it would
be healthier for us to live. He spent the whole summer scouting
around through north and west Texas and came on into this part of
Texas which had been given to Oklahoma by a Supreme Court decision.[12] He found a man that would sell him his improvements for
about $500 and relinquish his claim of one hundred and sixty acres
of land, embracing the Navajo Mountain and joining an inland
town of Navajo on the east.

   . . . My husband put up enough money to hold the trade and
came home to gather the crop and sell out our holdings and move
his family, which then consisted at that time of myself, his wife,
and seven children. I wanted more land and trusted my husband's
judgment but was a little afraid land so cheap would not be produc-
tive. We had been making a bale of cotton to the acre that year on
that fine black land where we lived. We had it about half gathered
as well as about half of the corn when November came and my
husband said, "Wife, we will have to go before it gets too cold for
the children." for he knew we would have to camp out of doors
several nights perhaps. We had some old neighbors . . . who had
been up here several years before and they had agreed to meet us
at Vernon, Texas. So we sold the balance of ungathered crop for
$200, about half of its worth, and our land for $200 an acre. We
chartered a car [railroad car]. We loaded the car with household
goods and over 500 one-half gallon jars of canned fruits and pre-
serves, our meat, lard, and other foods we always put up for the
winter use. Into this car we put two mules and one mare horse.
The children and I were put on the passenger train and our ticket
called for Vernon, Texas. There were several of our neighbors who
came along to scout the country. . . . When we got to Vernon, it
took us two days to load up and get ready to start but when we got
to the river, it was up. . . . I was afraid of quicksand and had made
Mr. H[—] promise that we would not ford the river. I had heard
too many tales of the quicksands of the Red River. I will never forget
the looks of that water to my dying day. I was used to the clear,
narrow rivers. Red River was so wide and the water just rolled
along so red and angry looking, it was the most frightful and

threatening thing I had ever seen. I thought, "I am going to a starvation land I am sure, but if I ever get across this stream safely I never, never under any circumstances want to come back across it. I will . . . stay in this new country." (80:357–61)

Anglo from Texas, b. none given

In the early days of Lawton, I came here with my mother and sisters on the train from Johnson County, Texas. My father and brothers drove a covered wagon, bringing cattle and our household things awhile before we came here.

. . . She [her mother] remembers seeing oxen pulling wagons to carry freight. The first car she saw was at a camp meeting at Wadesville. It created a great excitement. It looked like a turtle carrying his house.

. . . I never saw any roads, just little trails over the mountains to the little trading stores of Porum. (15:420)

Anglo, b. 1888

My parents moved to the Indian Territory in 1890 and settled twelve miles northeast of the present town of Duncan in Stephens County.

My father was very fortunate as he bought a lease from a Chickasaw Indian named Belton Colbert which was rather well improved.[13] He also bought a lease from an Indian woman by the name of Leewright and at last a lease from an Indian named Hahan.

Leases could be purchased very cheaply from these Indians for the white people would come in and take a ten year lease and stay as long as they wanted to or until they grew tired of the hardships of the country, and then they would sell out for anything they could get. Some times they would sell out for a cow, horse, or wagon and if they could not find a buyer for their claim, they would simply move out and leave what improvements they had put on the land. (41:463–64)

Anglo from Missouri, b. 1851

At the time of the opening of "Old Oklahoma" to settlement, we were living in Sumner County, Kansas. Mr. H[—] [her husband] was in the famous "Run," securing a good claim near Kingfisher.[14] After filing on the claim, Mr. H[—] came home. In August he went back to the claim, taking Milt, then sixteen years old, and me with him. Mr. H[—] started in to make some improvements. He plowed a few acres and set up some logs, stockade-fashion, for a house. This showed that we intended to make a home there. Then we went back to Kansas. In October, 1889, we loaded two wagons with things we would need most and went back to the claim, this time to stay. We took with us some chickens and two good cows; one of these cows died the first winter and the other the following spring. We thought their death was caused from eating too much dry feed. We surely missed the milk and butter as it was some time before we got another cow. Finally Mr. H[—] got a chance to trade a shotgun for a cow, which proved to be a good milker. Later that fall, Mr. H[—] went to Kansas bringing back feed for the stock, a pig, potatoes, and other food that we needed badly. By this time winter had set in and when he forded the Salt Fork River, he got stuck and had to leave the wagon in the river all night. The pig was in a crate on the back of the wagon, and cold as it was, Mr. H[—] waded to the wagon and fed it that night and the next morning. He stayed all night with some cowboys. (63:261–62)

Anglo from Illinois, b. 1864

On February 24, 1882, D[—] [interviewee] married W. H. H[—], in Leadville, Colorado, where they lived for one year, then they moved to Sumner County, Kansas; after living there three years they moved to Ford County, Kansas, and in July 1896, they came to Kay County, Oklahoma Territory, and traded their farm in Ford County, Kansas, for a quarter section of land eleven miles southwest of Tonkawa. Mr. H[—] was in the "race" when this Cherokee Outlet was opened to settlement . . . and secured a claim for a friend of his as Mr. H[—] was not eligible to hold a claim himself. . . .[15] (29:278)

Anglo from Ohio, b. 1862

We moved from Ohio to Indiana and then from Indiana to Illinois. We moved to a farm on the Illinois River, near a town called Seneca and we were there for quite awhile and then moved to a farm near Morse and Ottawa, Illinois, and we were there awhile and then moved again to a place near Chicago. These moves were made in covered wagons. . . . I was married to Mr. Emmet L[—], March 6, 1882, and went with him to live on a big ranch . . . in Harrison County, Missouri. . . . We came to Oklahoma in the fall after the opening, in 1889, and followed the old Chisholm Trail most if not all of the way.[16] We came from Kingman County, through Caldwell, Kansas, to Kiowa, then on to Driftwood Creek, about a day's drive from Kiowa, from there we passed Drums Ranch located in the Cherokee Strip, the last place before they got to Dover; from Dover we went to my father's farm which was located near Piedmont; my brother, my husband, our two small children, and I were in the party.[17]

We had two cows and the dog drove them all the way. We settled on an eighty acre farm south of Geary. It was a good farm with good timber on it and a great big dugout and a dugout barn. The dugout had a very large fireplace in it and we had plenty of wood to burn and I helped to saw and chop the wood we used in it. . . . We lived on this place about a year and a half, raising one crop and planting another and my husband got homesick to go back to Kansas and went; I of course followed him, and we let our nice home go back to the Government. We lived in Kansas a year, and then I came back to Oklahoma [divorced]. I cooked for a Mr. Hilton, the man who was supervisor of the Choctaw Railroad when it was under construction; I cooked on the average for about forty-five or fifty and I was in Geary when the first train came through that town; then I went to cook for a Mrs. Low who was running a boarding house in Geary and then I came to El Reno to run a boarding house of my own. . . .

I crossed the Cherokee Strip three of four times before it was
opened up, always in a covered wagon; as I crossed the great salt
plains, the salt would shine and sparkle in the sun, and people would
scoop the salt up by the scoop shovel and haul it away by the wagon
load. We lived right on the Chisholm Trail, but they called it the Kingman Trail then. I have seen freighters passing on it many times. . . .

My [second] husband freighted from Harper County to Kingman, Kansas. His team was a big roan and a large gray. I saw some
men freighting with ox teams in 1887. I saw a large herd of Texas
longhorns stampede in the Cherokee Strip and that was a sight to
see. (63:268–71)

Anglo from Illinois, b. 1855

Mr. R[—] drove a covered wagon with a stove, two chairs and
our bedding. The rest of the space was filled with farming implements and feed.

I drove a small covered spring wagon with the children. I had
coops of chickens and turkeys and a pen with two pigs in the back
of the wagon. I had two cages of canary birds fastened to the bows
on the inside. We carried our provisions, too.

Ahead of his wagon, Mr. R[—] drove nine cows. It was so
intensely hot that we had to leave them on pasture just before we
got to the Oklahoma line. After the first frost Mr. R[—] went back
after them.

We had to sleep under and in the wagons until we could build
a shelter. We cooked on our stove out in the open. It rained for so
long that our bedding was completely soaked.

We arrived on September 5th and on October 5th we buried
our oldest boy, Louis, aged eleven years. The three remaining children and my husband were all seriously ill with typhoid fever. I
did not become sick, however, and I nursed them for eight weeks.
(41:500–501)

Anglo, b. 1898

I came to Oklahoma with my parents when I was eleven
years old and there were only two white families near us for many

years. My parents came from Alabama to Holdenville in 1909. We came on the train and landed at 7 P.M. one night in January. There was snow and ice on the ground, and we had to get a man with a team and wagon to take us eleven miles to the place where my uncle lived, north of Holdenville. I remember that we were all very cold and part of the time, the horses were slipping around and the wagon also was slipping and going sideways. There was only one other white family near us. There was nothing to amuse us and no society of any kind. (80:270–71)

Anglo from Texas, b. 1869

I was married to my husband . . . in 1884 and 1887, he and his brother . . . came to Old Greer County for the purpose of securing land on which to build a home. They stopped on North Fork of Red River and in a short time I came also. I remember it very clearly for it was on my nineteenth birthday and our baby son, Charles, was seven months old. My mother-in-law, his mother, came with me, also his brother-in-law and sister. There was quite a family of us; we all lived together.

We remained at this place for a year, then moved to Lake Creek to our homestead which I still own. Part of the land I have divided among my eight children. (29:238)

Anglo from Texas, b. 1869

Just across the North Fork of Red River to the east in Indian Territory ran the Chisholm cattle trail and day after day great herds of cattle would be driven from Texas to Kansas, passing along this trail. It was not just once in a while but day after day. These herds would reach just as far to the south as we could see and just as far to the north, and would be a quarter of a mile wide. The Cattle Commission Companies hired men to stay along the line and "cut" herds.[18] These men were paid to watch these herds and take all of the cattle out of the herd which did not belong to it. Brands of the cattlemen were registered and these men had long lists of brands. . . . (62:197–98)

American Indian from Indian Territory, b. 1878

My mother when about eighteen years old came to this Indian country with a colony under Levi Kemp from Mississippi. She said they were driven like cattle coming over and treated very badly. They were two months on the way and many died. She often told me of a roaring that they could hear under the earth all the way over. They landed at Ft. Washita. (29:238)

American Indian from Alabama, b. 1868

Daddy was a judge in Okmulgee in the Indian Court or Council. I can remember his being gone for two or three weeks at a time. He went horse back by the ferry that was where the bridge is now at the Okmulgee Water Works. . . . He had black saddle-bags made of hair like sheepskin. We children were so tickled to see him and we would always run to these saddle bags for the candy he always brought to us.

One time I saw him cross on the ferry when the water was way flood high. They had to take broad axes and cut the limbs from the trees to let the boat pass. I don't see how they could take the boat across for there was no cable on that ferry. Sometimes he couldn't come home from Council because of high water . . . .

Two or three old ladies would go horseback to the McDermont Store, which was about twenty miles from our house. It was straight west, pass through a long prairie, on the other side of Okemah. It would take them all day and they just cut across, if there was a trail I don't know about it.

They would get their things in a sack and put it across the horse and ride back home, getting there about dark. (80:269–74)

American Indian, b. 1894

Tommy Yahola was my mother's father. When the Civil War came, he took my mother, who was about six years old and went north. He was a Northern soldier. Mother was uneducated.

Grandmother, Sowa, took Jennie Frank, mother's half sister, south to Waw-see-da. Aunt Jennie was quite a bit older than mother and a school teacher.

They didn't see each other till 1906. Jennie's girl, Mary, was on the train going to Sapulpa. My brother was on the same train and they got to talking. She told the story of how her mother had finally located her sister as living somewhere at Henryetta, but they didn't know exactly where. He told her that was his mother and where they lived. They both came to Henryetta the next day and went out to see mother, two miles North of Henryetta. She was so glad to see her and next day they all went to Sisocaway to see Aunt Jennie. (48:460)

Sac (Sauk) and Fox, b. none given

Most of the traveling was done on horseback. From the Sac and Fox Agency it was a two day trip to Cushing. People camped at those places where they found fresh water. (3:566)

Anglo from Missouri, b. 12-23-1885

I grew up in Missouri and we came to Geary, Oklahoma, in 1900. We made the trip on the train. I had a brother who lived in the country near Geary and at his continual insistence to come out to this wonderful country, we finally came. . . .

We lived in Geary for a few months after we were married. My husband was working for the Rock Island Railroad and they transferred him to Weatherford, then to Blackwell, and later he was transferred to Fort Worth, Texas. In 1908 we moved to El Reno. There were no street car lines here at the time. The Elks building had been brought here only a short time before we came, and the beautiful Methodist Church building, at the corner of Rock Island and Watts Streets was built very shortly after we came. The growth of El Reno has been gradual. In 1908, when we first came here, Fort Reno was a more important cog in the scheme of things than it is now, as there were more soldiers and more activity then there has been since it has been turned into a re-mount station. Most of the Fourth of July celebrations were held in Peaches Park, later, after the War, named Legion Park. We came here in the horse and buggy days and have watched the town grow up until it is fairly well streamlined. (85:98–100)

Cherokee from Georgia, b. 1840

The only ferry which I recall was the Government ferry across Grand River northwest of Fort Gibson which the soldiers used to haul freight over from Gibson Station at the railroad. Then there was Nevins ferry which crossed the Arkansas River at the mouth of Grand River and was run by Most and Julia Nevins. Most got killed one day in a drunken brawl down about the present Frisco depot at Fort Gibson, but Julia kept the ferry going for a long time after that.

The Junior Smith ferry crossed the Arkansas River about ten miles down stream from the Nevins ferry in the Gooseneck territory.

Rabbit Ford crossed the Arkansas River just east of Muskogee about four miles. (66:26–27)

Anglo from Indiana, b. 1864

The nearest railroad point to the H[—] home was Ponca City, a distance of twenty-five miles. No bus lines or other mode of public conveyance was then to be had. (29:284)

Anglo from Arkansas, b. 1860

Fort Smith, Arkansas was our principal trading point. However, with plenty of hogs and game for meat, our corn to be ground for meal, a small patch of cotton to provide funds with which to buy clothing and shoes, not many trips to "town" were necessary. As I look back over the years, I yearn for those days as they were years ago with their simple modes and the more intimate acquaintance of neighbors than we enjoy today. (4:181)

Anglo, b. none given

When the Cherokee Strip was thrown open for white settlement, he [her father] made the "run." I was four years old at the time and as I had been my father's almost constant companion since babyhood, he insisted on taking me with him on this trip. My mother was very apprehensive regarding the matter, but his will prevailed. We went to the little town of Kiowa [Kansas] and spent the night. The next morning everyone was lined up on the border waiting for the signal at 12:00 o'clock. By the firing of guns we started on the wild drive. My father was driving a good team hitched to a spring wagon. I stood on the front and held on to the dashboard. After traveling furiously for some time, he sighted a spot that he liked. He jumped from the wagon and I handed him the stakes and hammer and he drove the stakes into the ground while I held the horses. I was wearing a little dark blue calico dress and if I was wearing a bonnet, it must have been sewed on as that was the only way in which my mother succeeded in making me wear one.

We then went to the nearest land office where my father went through all the necessary preliminaries contingent to such matters as filing on a claim.

My older brother and sister also made the run and secured a claim several miles from my father's. (1:192)

Choctaw, b. Roebuck Lake, Choctaw Nation, Indian Territory

When the Choctaws reached Arkansas, the Government and wagons and teams there ready for them. The Indians were loaded into the wagons and they started for the Government post, near Little Rock, Arkansas.

In loading my people got separated from each other for there were hundreds of wagons on this journey. When they reached the Ouachita (meaning 4th River) River, it was on a rampage and out of banks. The roads were almost impassable. It was raining and cold. Even for the well and strong, the journey was almost beyond human endurance. Many were weak and broken-hearted, and as night came there were new graves dug beside the way. Many of the Indians contracted pneumonia fever and the cholera. They camped a mile from the Ouachita, waiting for the water to recede so they could cross. While they were camped here, Ezekiel Roebuck, father of my grandfather, William Roebuck, became ill but said nothing. When the river was low enough to cross, everyone got in the wagons and started on the journey but Ezekiel was so sick he became unconscious and fell over. Some one told the driver and he said, "I will have to stop and put him out as we can't afford to have any one with the Cholera along." So they stopped by the road side and put him out. My great-grandmother said, "You can put the children and me out too," and the driver replied, "All right, but he will soon be dead and you and your three children will have to walk the balance of the way." Each child had a small blanket.

My great-grandmother had a paisley shawl. She had also brought along a bucket of honey and some cold flour from their home. This flour is made by parching corn and grinding it in a coffee mill until pulverized. This food she carried along for her six months old baby. She begged the driver for food and a blanket for Great-grandfather, and he grudgingly gave the blanket and one day's supply of food.

Great-grandfather was conscious at times. He had dubbed Great-grandmother "Little Blue Hen" and when he became conscious of their plight, he would say, "Dear Little Blue Hen, why didn't you take the children and go on, I can't last much longer, and my Soul will rest much easier if I knew you were safe. My body is just dust and will be all right any place." She replied, "As long as you live I'll be with you, Dear." Then the Little Blue Hen and two boys, aged ten and twelve, set about fixing a bed. The boys had knives with which they cut the long stem grass until they made a fairly comfortable bed, then the three of them pulled the Father on it. They were fortunate to be where there was pine and the boys weren't long in gathering plenty of wood and pine knots; not only for warmth and lights but to keep hungry wolves and panthers away as they came circling around—growling and vicious looking. The boys threw up a high barricade behind their father's pallet, of brush, then a big fire a few feet in front and here the little family huddled together. They dared not let the fire die down until after day-break, then the beasts went back into the woods. When the Father became conscious, he praised the Little Blue Hen for her loyalty and he prayed that his little family might be spared from the dreaded disease. He only lived twenty-four hours after being put out of the wagon, and at sunset his soul passed on. The little Mother with sticks, and the boys with knives dug a grave deep enough to bury him, and piled rocks and dead trees on top of the grave to keep the beasts from the body. Then the boys blazed the trees all around the grave. They wanted to leave the grave well marked for they intended to return for their father's body some day. They fed on roots, wild berries, a spoonful of honey and a small portion of the cold flour and the next morning the brave mother with her three children bade farewell to the Honey King's grave, by the roadside of the Trail of Tears, and they traveled on to the post, following the wagon tracks to the river, which they realized they would have to swim across. Undaunted she took her paisley shawl and tied the baby onto her back and cautioning her boys to stay close to her they all swam across the river. Here they found the wagon tracks, but they stopped long enough to build a big fire and dry their clothes. They then walked all the way to the Government Post, where they were given food, clothes and shelter. The next day they were carried to the border line in a wagon and from there they walked all the way into Doaksville, where Captain Doaks gave them plenty to eat and clean clothing. They rested here several days. Captain Doaks sent word to her uncle, David Folsom, and he came for her and took her and children down to the Kiamichi. (33:49–54)

TWO

Making a Home

In southwestern Oklahoma, the Plains Indians dwelt in teepees. By contrast, the removed tribes constructed their homes much like those they had left behind in the South, except for the Seminoles, who had abandoned materials native to Florida swamps for local timber. The early houses of the Five Tribes were made from logs nailed together and then chinked with clay. Because often the unseasoned timber shrank, native clay made up much of the dwellings. Small sticks and hides served as shutters, split logs and hides as doors. Later doors were imported by wagon from Texas and Arkansas.[1]

As the years passed, Indian Territory boasted structures worthy of eastern dwellings. A significant town in Choctaw Nation, Boggy Depot possessed several fine houses, one of which was a t-structure with two stories for the crosspiece and a single story for the long arm of the t. Wide, covered porches stretched across the entire front of the house.[2] It is probable that Lena lived with her white Texan husband in a somewhat simpler t-structure.

In eastern Indian Territory, wealthy Indians built plantation-style homes. For those not of the plantation class, dogtrot houses and shotgun houses were built after sawmills were established.[3] Floors were plank, dirt, or a mixture of both. When an addition became necessary, a lean-to was constructed.

When Indian Territory was opened to white settlement in 1889, whites dwelt in structures like those of American Indians. At first many families lived in tents because outbuildings such as smokehouses and barns were often built first. In addition to log houses common in the timbered areas, further west the people constructed dugouts by digging into the sides of hills or plowed the soil into brick-shaped sections for sod houses. Shingles were made of split wood, and, in early sod houses and dugouts, often sheets of sod like shingles were laid over sticks for roofing. Newspapers made good wallpaper.

Most settlers lived with several family members in dwellings described as 16 x 18 feet or 10 x 12 feet, a room or two. In the land run areas, tent cities grew up overnight, and housing materials consisted of anything that pioneers could drape with blankets or wagon covers. Railroads brought in homes built in sections for quick assembly to those who could afford them, and some settlers brought their own lumber for building. A few people disassembled houses, numbered the materials, and brought the coded materials with them. As time passed, abandoned homes were recycled into new structures in new locations.

Within all structures the women tried to make a comfortable and even gracious life. Members of the Five Tribes brought what furniture they could, but most of them had to build it after arrival in Indian Territory. The wealthy members of the Five Tribes imported their furnishings and wallpaper. In the earlier days of white settlement, furniture and cooking appliances were limited for the lower socioeconomic class. Beds were built into walls of dugouts and propped with wood, and cooking was done in fireplaces or on outside fires. Basic kitchen equipment consisted of a coffee pot, a Dutch oven, and a skillet. Dishes and cutlery were simple, except in wealthier homes. Women made their bedclothes, made and repaired all the family's clothing, and laundered outside, using lye soap and washpots. Early on, fires were made using flint and tinder; kerosene lamps, and candles were household necessities. By 1907 electricity was available to those who had access and money.

Clearly, women were interested in a pleasant life rather than one of mere subsistence, because gracious living required more work, and women went to the trouble to create beauty in their homes. However, women who lived away from towns existed in isolation in their homes, communicating only with their families and nearby neighbors. Newspapers were available to pioneer women of the Five Tribes, and it must be presumed that some of them read those papers.

In Indian Territory the tribes early established newspapers, such as the *Cherokee Phoenix,* which was brought in 1837 to Park Hill and was printed both in English and Cherokee. Telephones came later and at first were available only on a very limited basis. The telephone was invented in 1876 and came to Darlington, Oklahoma, in the territory's western region in 1884. The Darlington line ran to a telegraph connection in Fort Reno. In northeastern Indian Territory, a telephone line that ran from Tahlequah to Muskogee was established two years later.[4] Still, away from these towns telephone access did not exist for many years. Thus isolation was a way of life on the farms and ranches.

Anglo from Texas, b. 11-9-1877

This was May time of the year. You see uncle had our dugout ready for us and land fenced and crop planted. There was no shed or wind break of any kind for the stock. We lived in our tent until lumber could be hauled from Quanah and Chillicothe, Texas, to build a two room house. Our tent was nice and large and we could put up beds and get out our chairs and live just like you would in a house. (89:66)

Anglo from Tennessee, b. 1890

But anyway we came on over and put up two tents and a smoke house and lived in those until Papa got our house built. You see he had brought five loads of lumber with us when we came and he put up the first residence that was ever built in the town of Boswell. That house is standing today. A story and a half high. (89:98)

Anglo from Texas, b. 1881

Father told us all the good things about the place he could think of but we were not prepared for the log house. We had seen log houses but they were made of great big logs and were airy and light. This house more properly could be called a pole house as the trees it was built out of were small and all the cracks were daubed with mud and grasses and the roof was of mud and grass. This log hut was only one big room, while there was a half dugout that we had to use for cooking and eating.

Mother never got reconciled to her house and only lived two years. There was an abundance of good, pure water but that would not take the place of a house. (89:110)

Anglo from Kansas, b. 6-14-1886

We built a barn fourteen feet wide by thirty feet long, putting regular barn doors in the ends and windows on the south side of the building; it was just a box affair, but we lived in it from August, 1892, until the next spring, when we moved into a dugout that we had constructed in the winter time. We lived in this dugout until we got our five room house built, which was not for very long. (89:159–60)

Anglo, b. 1-17-1869

As we were too late to get a homestead, we settled on school land, which we really had no right to do, for at that time there was no law regarding what should be done with school land, whether it should be put up and sold to the highest bidder on forty years time or leased for a number of years to the highest bidder, and we also took a chance of being put off of the land by soldiers at any time.

This school land was about four miles south and two miles west of the present city of Yukon, which was not in existence at that time. There was no way at that time of leasing school land; you just squatted on it and hoped to be permitted to stay. The soldiers could come and put you off it, if you did something displeasing to them, such as cutting timber or anything else that they thought might be detrimental to the value of the property.

And so, since money was scarce and everything uncertain, how long we might be permitted to stay, our buildings were put up as cheaply as possible. Our house half dugout and half lumber, with two half windows, one in the north end one in the south, with a door in the east. Bank barn or stables (dug out of a bank) and a bank chicken house. A good dug well of water close to the house. Every little while we would hear that the soldiers were putting the settlers or squatters off the school land. (12:218–19)

Anglo from Texas, b. 1889

My husband and his brother, Charles, made a dugout for us to live in and built a picket house of one room a short distance away. The dugout was made by digging down in the side of a bank for several feet and was then covered over with bark and on top of that was piled dirt. I did not like the dirt falling down through the cracks, so I lined the walls and ceiling with newspapers. This helped a good deal, but we could hear bugs and centipedes crawling behind the paper. I would push the scissors through and often cut the centipedes in two or kill the spiders. . . . The rattlesnakes were the worst thing to contend with, for they were so numerous and poisonous, we had to be constantly on the lookout for them.

. . . My husband, his mother, his sister, and her husband, our baby and I and the four men boarders all lived in the dugout and picket house that year. The family lived in the dugout and the men had the picket house to themselves. It does not seem to me now that we were crowded. We were happy. (62:197–98)

Anglo, b. 1888

If a person bought a lease, he or she would finish out the remainder of the ten years residence which were [sic] required. Father bought this Hahan lease, and it only had two years on it. The house was a good boxed two rooms in front with a shed room running the full length. We were proud of this house for it was the best in the country and had a shingle roof. Almost everybody else lived in a log house or in a dugout. (41:464)

Anglo from Texas, b. 1874

In nine years I made six feather beds and twenty-two pillows from geese I raised. Now, that took many a picking, and many a step. Feathers must be sunned almost daily for at least six months in thin sacks in order to "cure" them. Sun them hanging. If feathers are put in thick ticking "green" they will smell like something dead, just as long as they are in a bed or a pillow. I tramped many a mile in these woods after my geese, and earned all I got out of them, but we pioneer women never thought of anything else but working and doing our share. (43:229)

Anglo, b. 1851

At first we lived in a tent borrowed from a neighbor who had built a house, so he could spare his tent to us. However, we soon had our log house ready to live in. It was big enough for two rooms, but we did not partition it for some time. Everyone felt the need of a Sunday school and as our house afforded the most room, the people of the community met there each Sunday for nearly a year. (63:259)

Anglo, b. 1860

In Muskokee country, we built our houses out of split logs, standing up these split logs all around I guess about ten feet wide and twelve feet long, daubed with gray or red clay, and we covered these houses with hickory tree bark. After this bark gets dry, it is as good as cement they are using today. (21:263-64)

Anglo from Indiana, b. 1864

The one hundred and sixty acres that Mr. and Mrs. H[—] had traded for in this new country had no improvements upon it except a small "dugout" on the east side of the place and a well of water on the west side, and thirty acres of land which had been put in cultivation. Immediately after trading for this land they bought a four room house in Wellington, Kansas, and carefully tore it down, saving every board that came out of it and every nail; they hauled it a distance of sixty miles to their farm and rebuilt it, every piece of timber being fitted back in its former position in the building, except the lath which held the plaster, as they lost the plaster and were unable at that time to buy new plaster to finish it, but they did plaster it a year later.

They gave a workman a horse to help them tear down and rebuild this house. (29:277, 284)

Anglo, b. none given

As building material was scarce and hard to get, it was necessary for many people to live in dugouts. Ours was builded [sic] into a side of a hill, with the front made of lumber. It was a large room 16 x 18 feet, perfectly comfortable and absolutely secure from the wind storm which was so prevalent in that section of the country. We had plenty of light as we had nice glass windows on the front. That was the home in which I was born and in which my parents lived with their nine children. (1:192)

Anglo from Texas, b. 1857

When we got across the river, we camped right there for the night and during the night there came the blowingest and coldest wind I had ever known. We could not have a fire for coffee. We went to the nearest dugout and asked the privilege of making coffee on their fire. We were all invited in for breakfast and I want to say before I forget it, that was the nicest, cleanest home I ever saw.

I never dreamed that a dirt floor and a hole in the ground could look so cozy and home-like. It allayed my uneasiness about the country a little. If that lady could be so happy, nice and clean in a dugout, surely I could make a home when I knew I was to have a four room house and be real near a town where there was a good school.

As we started on north, the land surely did look bare and desolate at that time of the year. We got to Navajo about three o'clock in the afternoon. Lady Estes, the one we were buying from, had a good dinner waiting for us.

With the shack that was on the place my husband planned to add to it and make four rooms for us. It was a crude house and not very warm, but good for this country at that time. Everyone was busy with their own home making, so we could not get anyone to help with the new house. At last a man was found that was not a carpenter but claimed he knew a little about building. He said he would help for $10.00 a day, and as it was the best we could, we had to pay it. At that it was nearly three months before the new house was ready for us to move into. All posts and joists were hauled from the Indian Reservation.[1] It took a man two days to go to Vernon and back with a load of lumber. (80:360–61)

Anglo from Texas, b. 1889

Father built us a log house, two large rooms 20 x 30 placed so that there was a space in between which was roofed over and we cooked in this shed or porch between the two rooms. The two rooms on either side were used for bedrooms, and each of them had a fireplace, for stoves were scarce in those days. At first we cooked on a fireplace.

. . . That was true contentment; our family were [sic] closer to each other and each one's troubles was the concern of the whole family. There was no rush hither and thither, one member going to a party fifty miles in one direction and another to church a few blocks away, another to a picture show, and some other member to a political meeting. When we went to a picnic or fishing, the whole family went. A new dress for one of the women or a shirt for one of the boys meant something to us all. There is no happiness without contentment, and we had it. Mother knit our stockings and gloves, and we women folks sewed on our fingers for the family.

Some years later we got a sewing machine; that was a great event in our family. (100:404)

Anglo, b. 1874

[T]hen the hard times began. El Reno was the nearest railroad town, a distance of about one hundred and fifty miles. We were here with no material to build houses, but we lived in tents and the men soon set about houses. Some of them were built of cottonwood logs that grew in canyons about twelve miles from where we were, and it was no easy task to cut those logs and drag them out of the canyons. Of course, this had to be done with horses, and then hauled to our claims over the prairie where the grass was waist high and there were no roads.

My father's house in the Territory was dug down in the ground and walled up with logs and covered with logs and dirt. There was only one house from Hammon to Ural; it was a little shanty over on Elk Creek and it was for sale. I begged my father to buy it for I thought I could never go to sleep in a dugout. But by the time the dugout was done, we were glad to get in it. It had a board door and a fireplace in one end and we cooked on the fireplace for a while. . . . (85:81)

Anglo from Texas, b. 1869

We were, as a rule, very healthy, but one time Mother had pneumonia and our nearest neighbors were four and seven miles. One of them went sixty miles to a doctor for medicine. The doctor came and stayed a week until Mother was out of danger. We never had a doctor for confinement cases; the women of the neighborhood took care of each other. (100:404–12)

Anglo, b. 1855

All mail had to be called for at Quanah, but every time any one from the neighborhood went, they took all the names and called for the mail for each one who lived in a radius of twelve miles. That way we heard from the post office real often. . . . (72:338–39)

Euchee Creek, 88 years

In those days they had what was known as squaw corn and that was their flour. They took the corn and beat it up and made flour for their meals and they would use the corn in many different ways. Such as Hominy, and they would take the corn, cook it with the wild game they kill. They also had what was known among Indians, the Indian sweet potato. But the potatoes are all out. [handwritten comment: Jesse Allen (Uchee) 89 yrs. has these potatoes. This species of potato appears to belong to the Uchee-Creeks.] Now days the Indians when they raised the corn, they had a wooden block which had a hole in it; the block was made of the best of wood and it was hickory wood and also there was a pestle to ground [sic] the corn. The woman would do the pounding of the corn in those days. The Indians did not have any pans. They made their bowls out of wood [handwritten: box elderwood] and also they did not have any spoon. They had what was known as Dutch oven in that time. [handwritten comment: The cast-iron oven used by white pioneers and cowboys] They used the Dutch as a bread pan. They would put the corn meal in the oven and put lid on it and bake it in the fire and they would put hot coals of fire on it and bake the bread. And the potatoes and Indians would cut them in half and dry them out in the sun and put them up for the winter, and they would cook green roast ears corn on cobbs [sic] and after the corn was cooked, they take them and dry them out on cobbs and after they are dry, they would shell and put them away for winter use. That was what Fannie F[—] said that was the way the old time Indian put up their stuff to eat.

She said she was about 12 years old at the time of the Civil War. Her father was killed in that war at the time. This is all she would tell me. (3:614–15)

[The field worker is directed to obtain more information.]

Choctaw, b. none given

Our houses were made of logs hewed and put together neatly. There were not many conveniences, but we were comfortable. We had plenty to eat for there was an abundance of wild meat and we raised our corn and vegetables. Our surplus crop was sold at Fort Smith. We bought clothing, shoes, and such food as we could not raise on the farm.

. . .

We had all the good things we could eat. There was the hickory nut hominy. Nothing could be better; and parched corn; and the beaten bread, and so many other good things. I have made them often since I have been a woman, but none of them have ever tasted so good as they did when I was a child.

I am old now and have lived a full life, but those good old days when I was a child are still dear to me, and the memory of them brighten many a day that otherwise would be dreary. (25:253–54, 256)

Anglo from Illinois, b. 1855

When Mr. R[—] [interviewee's husband] was able we placed some poles in the ground and thatched two sides with brush and grass. Two sides were open. On one side I hung an old carpet and put an old bed sheet on the other. It leaked terribly bad [sic]. This protection was all we had for a while.

Mr. R[—] had a relapse [typhoid] and never was completely well during the rest of his life. The neighbors gathered and built us a 12 x 13 one roomed [sic] log cabin. My sister sent me enough money to put in two windows, a door, and the floor. The boys of the neighborhood made our furniture which consisted of table, three stools made of split logs, a corner cupboard, and beds. The beds were built bunk fashion for the children.

We moved in on Monday, and the next Monday, my little girl Maud was born. (41:501)

Anglo, b. 1862 Columbus, Ohio

It was my experience with the fullblood [sic] Choctaw tribe in this country in the early day that they did make very good neighbors to the white settlers. They very seldom visited with the whites. They seemed to just stay around their own cabins . . . . (63:268–69)

Anglo from Texas, b. 1869

The Kiowa Indians came over every day. I never feared them. Komalta and his tribe came often. One time more than one hundred came by on their way home from a picnic which they had attended at Mangum; this was about 1899.[2]

We had good neighbors and enjoyed many things among ourselves. The Castle family were quite musical . . . all of whom played musical instruments. (62:200)

Delaware, b. none given

When we first arrived in the Indian Territory, we camped in the Forks of Caney for awhile, then moved about one and one-half miles south of Bartlesville on what is now Highway 75.

My parents were each allotted 160 acres and my father bought a house for $30.00 and we lived in this house for a while, then moved to a log house, which had one long room, where we lived for two years. When I was about 15 years old, my father built a seven room frame house. We children all grew to manhood and womanhood in this house. Our family have lived on this place for sixty years and my brother George's widow, Mrs. Katie Whiteturkey, lives there at the present. (2:471)

Anglo, b. none given

Our house was a log shack with two rooms. One room had a floor, which was made of native lumber and there were large cracks between the boards. We nearly froze to death in the winter. We had a fireplace, the lower part being made of rock, and the upper part of sticks and dirt. The other room had a dirt floor. (80:99)

Euchee, b. none given

[The interviewee] says that the Indians back times how they farmed. The Indians in those days did not have any farming tools. In that time the only things they had for tools was a plough made out of wood that had a big fork in it and for their teams were oxen. They would use the oxen and farm their land and raise their crops. (3:614)

Anglo from Russia, b. 8-30-1884

I worked for about ten years in the Quanah Parker home.

. . .

There are thirteen rooms in the Quanah Parker house. It has been said that the lumber for this house was hauled from Vernon, Texas, nearly forty-three years ago. Several of Quanah Parker's wives are living, but none of them live in this home; a daughter lives there. One wife (Topay) lives about one mile east of the home place and one lives one mile north of Apache. (26:149)

Anglo, b. none given

[We moved] to a place on a hill above Turtle Lake; the hill was covered with pines. We had a big log smoke house there, and we kept it full of meat all the time; beef and pork, but mostly pork, smoked and salted.

My father owned some cattle and lots of hogs, I remember his going out and marking the ears of the hogs. (89:26)

Anglo from Tennessee, b. 1-18-1870, parents from England

There was one store there and we called it the Coffee Store, for the man kept very few things other than coffee, though as I was to later find out that was about all that was necessary for a grocery-man to keep in store for people lived principally on corn bread, black coffee, beef and wild game such as turkey and deer. (89:36)

Anglo from Texas, b. 1897

We had a good well of water and a windmill. The neighbors got water from our place. Some people in the community didn't have enough water for home use.

We burned wood and a little coal, getting the coal at Rocky [illegible] where we also got our groceries. (89:2)

Anglo from Texas, b. 1881

This was truly a goodly land. Everything would grow. There was such a good garden. Father traded around and got some more pigs and cows so there was plenty of milk and butter and good pork meat. A big crop of corn and cane was raised and some cotton. We had our chickens already. School and church were held about a mile away in a little frame building. We always walked. All the denominations preached in the same building the school was held in, each denomination taking a Sunday about. There was a Union Sunday school that everyone, young and old, rich and poor, attended every Sunday but Mother could not get over the awful house we lived in. We brought a safe for our dishes and a wardrobe for our clothes and we also had a sewing machine. Sweet potatoes and sorghum syrup were always on the table. The woods were full of nuts, pecans, hickory nuts and walnuts to be had for the gathering and I must not forget persimmons for we used them in many ways. Father cut all the wood we needed for fuel right on the place where we lived. This place was about thirty-five miles from Duncan near a little place called Loco. (89:113–14)

Anglo from Kansas, b. 6-15-1886

My mother brought a lot of dried fruit, canned fruit and other things with us from Kansas; she also brought a lot of house plants. The plants were a lot of care, as the house we lived in was large and airy and thin walled. She had to put them on the table and keep them well covered with blankets, in cold weather, to keep them from freezing. Mother never lost any of her house plants, however, by freezing. We could raise all kinds of garden stuff, as well as corn and kaffir corn and we raised some of the loveliest watermelons. They were the white, thin-skinned kind. They were very large, skins thin and white, inside red and luscious, and we raised lots of them. (89:159)

Anglo from Iowa, b. 4-5-1872, parents from Indiana

There were lots of wild plums, and grapes on the South Canadian River, which I gathered every fall and made into jelly. We lived in Mineo until 1902. (12:462)

Cherokee, b. 3-17-1864 Thomasville, Georgia

Although we were Cherokee Indians, we didn't come into the Territory until 1882. My father, Mat Williams, had come out and gone into the cattle business, his ranch being on Coody Creek, east of Muskogee, where he had a big ranch and grazed a big herd of cattle. He wanted us to come West, so my mother bundled us up and we came out to Muskogee. This was in 1882. We lived in Muskogee, never living out on the ranch. While we were Cherokee Indians, we had been used to a quiet and secure existence so the wild new country frightened my mother and she preferred to live in town. (12:426)

Anglo, b. 9-28-1855 Jay County, Indiana

During the early days we had friends to visit us from the eastern states but it was very seldom they ever saw an Indian and they felt so afraid of them. I always managed to take them to Darlington to see the Indians and to visit their camps. Most of the Indians knew me and when we came into their camp they would all gather around me patting me on the back, all talking in their native language, all at the same time. My friends would draw back from the crowd and they often told me they were ready to run. However, I always explained that they were good people and some of my best friends were Indians and are even today. I have Indian friends who come to visit me and spend a week at a time in my home.

My eastern friends often went down to the North Canadian River on a hot summer afternoon to watch the Indians who were camped up and down the river. We often sat on the river banks for hours watching the Indians teach their young children to swim. They would take the child from one year and a half or two years old, pick it up throw it in the river and tell it to swim. The little fellows would always manage to reach the bank and the parents would let the child rest, then throw it back in again. Sometimes they would throw twigs in the river and tell the children to bring it to them. We have witnessed this event when the river would be up and even men would be afraid to swim it.

My friends thought the beef issues were the cruelest things they had ever witnessed. At these beef issues the cattle stood in the pens twelve hours before the slaughter and the Indians would inspect the cattle and make their selections.[3] As soon as they were released, the bucks would chase them on horseback, shooting at them.

When we left our old home in Coalwater, Ohio, I was very sad and felt that if I traveled the world over I could never find a place I would like as well. But today, in our nice old home which we have lived in for twenty years, I can truly say I am enjoying living in El Reno and Canadian County as well. (12:104–105, 107)

Choctaw, b. 1881 Pushmataha County

Father and Mother farmed. They raised lots of corn, cotton, hogs, cattle and sheep. We had no fenced pastures but there was lots of good tall grass and the stock ran on the range. Father had four ponies.

When Father went hunting he would kill one deer and no more. He would skin it where he killed it and put it on the horse and carry it home. We often cut our hams in thin slices and put it on top of the house to dry; and used it as needed. It was very easy to cook. Our principal foods were pashofa, chuck bread, sour bread and dried corn.[4]

We had our tents, blankets and quilts. This was at our summer camp meeting where we stayed for two or three days at a time. Each family cooked themselves and had their own meals alone. No whites ever attended these meetings that I remember of.

Father went [to] Fort Smith, Arkansas, to buy his guns and ammunition. He would be gone a week. I never went on these trips; however, I never went any place, I stayed very close at home and knew very little of what the other people were doing or their ways of living.

I don't remember how we made our medicines but I do know we used lots of home remedies. I never attended the Pashofa dances but do know they had them as well as the three day cries.[5]

Our clothes were home made. My mother used to spin the thread and weave the cloth but never taught me how. The men wore their hair to their shoulders while the women wore it long, down each shoulder in a braid.

My husband was a Baptist Missionary Minister, preaching in the Indian Territory. (31:125–26)

Anglo, b. 1867

We settled about four miles south of Altus. This was the year of the flood, and the town of old Frazier was being moved from near Bitter Creek to the present site of Altus. We bought one of the small houses that were being moved and used it on our place. We homesteaded one hundred and sixty acres, and later bought another quarter section for a dollar an acre with five years to pay.

. . .

I made a trip to Mineral Wells to visit friends, and stayed several weeks. That must have been some thirty years ago. During my absence, Mr. J[—] [her husband] remodeled and redecorated the house. We were living in Altus at that time. The night we returned from the trip we found the house brilliantly lighted with electricity. I thought then, that our home was the most beautiful place I had ever seen. (31:161–63)

Anglo, b. 10-16-1856 Indianapolis, Indiana

We leased some land from a squaw man by the name of Melott and on it we built a one room log cabin chinked and daubed with a stick and mud chimney for heating. There was a sawmill on Pont Creek and there we got native lumber to make the roof and doors to our cabin.

Most all the neighbors we had were our kinfolks and the country was so wild that we women were afraid all the time when we camped out; I was afraid of animals and snakes as well as of the Indians, negroes, and lots of the white people.

My father went back to Texas after some time but we continued to farm raising mostly corn and a little cotton. A gin was built at Elk and a store and blacksmith shop were built. (31:272A)

Anglo from Kentucky, b. 11-8-1867

We farmed a little, raised gardens and had an orchard. These vegetables and fruits I would divide with my neighbors. I also gave my neighbors milk and butter, and was glad I had a good supply so I could divide.

I was afraid to stay alone. One day I had two Indian women callers. I tried to entertain my callers so I got my pictures out of my trunk for them to see. They would smile, grunt and point. Soon they wondered how we cooked and looked at our food. They would like to taste our food.

One day an Indian man came riding up in the yard. Wanted beef, wanted beef, wanted to see my side saddle, that I had brought from Texas with me. I was so frightened I ran to a neighbor's house almost a mile away.

I learned very early that the wind blew very hard here, blowing my tents almost away one morning before breakfast. Then I decided if I stayed here, I needed a house that would stand up to this strong wind. The two tents served as our entire house. One was a kitchen and dining room, the other tent served as our bed and living room.

We bought lumber from Lawton and built our home which was located on Blue Beaver Creek about fifteen miles from Lawton. (37:266–68)

Choctaw freedwoman, b. about 1857

I live here in this old shack alone. There was a log house here first but it was about to fall down on me, so I got this second hand house and had it put here. It was not much house to begin with, but it has been here about forty years. An old negro, named Matt

Freeman, made the boards for the roof when we first re-built it here, about forty years ago. He is about ninety years old now and lives at Sawyer.

. . .

I had my log house built here long before we filed on any land. Then, after the Choctaws adopted us negroes and said we could have forty acres of land, I went to the Sulphur Springs Court at Alikshi, where they were filing the Indians and negroes, and I filed on this land and still have the most it.[6] It will be my home when I die. (31:49–50)

Chickasaw, b. none given

My mother was a Cherokee. I was born in Arkansas and moved with my parents near Caddo in the Caddo hills.

I remember my grandmother lived with us and at night she would help put us children to bed and would always warm a linsey wool quilt before the fire before spreading it over us.

I used to hoe in the garden with my grandmother. She always wore her hoops, even when working in the garden; the only time she did not wear them, was when it was stormy; she said the steel would draw lightning. My sister and I made her a pair of hoops from briar branches, cutting the briars off.

We beat our hominy meal for breakfast. Everyone at our house was up at four in the morning. One morning I was pushing corn in the hopper and sister was beating it with a pestle and she hit me on the head nearly killing me and another time she accidentally cut my head open with a hoe when I stepped in front of her while she was chopping corn. I nearly bled to death before they got a doctor to sew the wound up.

. . .

When I was married my husband took me to a little log house he had prepared for me; the floor was made of split logs; our bed was a scaffold, with one leg, built in the corner. We used oxen to plow with and made our own tools to work with.

. . .

I used to make pets out of the little fawn and they would stay around the house with the stock. I had planted some beans and I told my husband I guessed the rabbits were eating them but we watched and it was my pet fawns.

Turkeys were so fat that one day my husband killed one and it fell into the creek and the skin popped open.

I spun and made my clothes, but when I was married and tried to make my husband a pair of pants, I almost wore the pocket out trying to sew it in. I made soap and never knew what it was to buy it; I helped saw timber and worked in the field. I have helped lay many a rail fence.

We always used spring water, and had a barrel in which to catch rain water. I used flint to start my fire and many times I have knocked the skillet with a knife and put a piece of cotton on top so it would catch the spark. I "broke" cows for the use of the milk and some of them were so wild that I would tie them and then milk them through the rail fence; they kicked like mules.

I rode horseback up until 1905 and many times I have had my face skinned when my horse would run away through the timber jumping creeks as he went.

· · ·

Our chimney to the house was built of sticks and dirt and there were many holes between the logs and chimney. I was sitting there spinning, barefooted, one evening when I heard a rattling and looked up to see a large rattlesnake that was ready to spring on me. I ran for a hoe and killed it. (12:171–75)

Anglo from Illinois, b. 1861

When we came to Oklahoma the next spring after the opening we chartered a car [railroad car] and brought everything we owned to the new state [note: Oklahoma statehood occurs in 1907]. We put our furniture, feed, horses, cows, pigs, wagons, implements and buggy all in the car. It came to Perry. We decided we didn't want to locate in Perry so as soon as the car arrived in Perry, my husband loaded the wagons with as much as he could and drove to Pawnee. The smaller children and I came over on the stage. We got a room in Pawnee and stayed there about a week. It took about a week to get everything moved over there, then we moved on to Blackburn in the same way. We had lived in Blackburn only a short time when Mr. M[—] [her husband] bought a quarter section of land just southwest of Osage City.[7] He gave $1000 for it without any improvements. Mr. M[—] then freighted lumber from Perry to build a house before we moved from Blackburn. There was only one other frame building in the neighborhood. This was a little one room building with an upstairs and was owned by Mr. Carmen. He had asthma and was told not to live in a dug-out as most of the other people around there did.

I brought a barrel of home-made soap with me to Oklahoma, made with ashes. As soon as we were well established Mr. M[—] made me a hopper. This was a V-shaped board frame about four feet long and two feet wide at the top. It set close to the ground. In this wood ashes were packed all winter. When I got ready to make soap, I would put my grease and meat scraps in a big iron kettle out doors. Water was poured on the packed ashes in the hopper and as it slowly seeped through it took up the lye. This content of the ashes was collected as it ran out and poured on the grease, then the mixture was cooked to the right consistency for soap.

Just before coming to Oklahoma Mr. M[—] bought our oldest son, Oscar, then twenty-six years old, a new two horse buggy. When we got to the new state, this was the only buggy anywhere around and when Mr. M[—] was buried in 1900, it was the only buggy in the long procession. One of the young men in the neighborhood made a two wheel cart by using two wagon wheels, making a small box bed for them and a spring wagon seat for the seat. Aside from these everyone went either horseback or in the lumber wagon. (37:126–27)

Anglo from Texas, b. 1899

My father and the boys did all the farming with mules and two ponies. The only implements they had for many years were a plow, a harrow they made themselves, and a scythe. They raised corn and cotton.

My father was known as a good provider. We had milk and butter from the cows we got from the cattlemen in that section of the country; Father did not own any for many years. One time we got out of flour and we just had biscuits for Sunday morning breakfast for about six weeks, when Father made one of those long trips to Gainesville, Texas, for a six months' supply of necessary things.

We got our news from the outlaws who came across the river to escape the officers. They told us what they knew about the outside world, and, as far as they were concerned, we asked no questions. You can easily see that this information would depend greatly upon the education, environment, and associations of the person from whom we received the news. (100:405–407)

Anglo from Texas, b. 1857

We bought corn for fifty cents a bushel for the stock. The ears were four or five inches long and about two or three inches around, and I thought it was not fit to feed the chickens with. It did not look good to me. Mr. H[—] [her husband] bought some cows and we had a lot of milk and butter, but I did not like the taste of the milk very much; it tasted too weedy. . . . Some of the cattle were so wild that they had to be roped and tied down every time they were milked, which was a great nuisance, but they were hardy and thrived well. . . . There was a beef club that killed a yearling every week and you got your part of the beef. You furnished a yearling whenever your time came and took different parts of the beef until you had had a whole beef and then started over again. We were never without beef and I am tired of beef yet. We put out a berry patch and an orchard at once. . . . We put out Austin dewberries and gathered twenty-eight gallons one morning from our patch. . . . Watermelons kept so well we sometimes had watermelon for Christmas dinner. . . . Mules did well and we could get $300.00 for a span for good gentled mules. Hogs were not worth much and did not do so well either. They were always having the cholera or something. If we did not sell so many hogs, we always had plenty of cured meat and lard for the family. . . . Our orchards were always good, but we had to plant over often for the hail or wind was for-ever killing the trees. There was never much market for such stuff.

People came to the orchard and helped themselves. They also came to the melon patch and hauled away what they wanted. I have sold eggs for as little as two cents a dozen and have given lots of butter away, for it was worth nothing at all. No one ever thought of trying to sell a chicken—there were too many wild turkeys and prairie chickens in the country.

We have given as high as $4.00 per day and board for cotton choppers and believe me, we fed them well. . . .

The things we most feared were rattlesnakes, black smallpox, and typhoid fever. . . .

I think the thing that gave me the most trouble was cooking with green wood before we could get coal. . . . (80:362–66)

Anglo, b. 1856

The camp was soon started and all were busy getting our half dugout started. We built two dugouts, one for the kitchen and one for a place to sleep. These just had covers; they had no wood floors.

The next thing was to get water of some kind and in some way, so the men dug a well by hand. And the water they got was pure gyp which was not good in any sense of the word. The water had to be drawn up in buckets for the stock as well as for house-hold purposes, and later we got a crank and rope, and we could wind the crank and draw water that way, which was a great help.

In 1897 we raised eight bales of cotton and hauled it to Qua-nah which was our trading post and we received four cents per pound for it. We also raised millet and sorghum.

For food we had our chickens and cows so you see we had eggs and milk and butter.

We made hominy, using wood ashes for the lye. Then we could go out and kill quail, wild turkey, antelope, and deer. And we also raised sweet potatoes. To cook the potatoes we would bury them in hot ashes at night to bake and the next morning they were fine.

The cooking vessels we used were not like those of today [1937]. We had everything iron. (104:108)

Anglo, b. 1855

Mr. B[—] got me a wood cook stove in Quanah for he was tired of me cooking over an open fire.

In the summer of 1890 my husband, with the help of some neighbors who lived near us, dug our hole in the ground. They hauled lumber from Quanah to make a half dugout 14 x 16 feet. We had two windows of glass and the dugout was divided into two rooms with a rock fireplace in one end. The rocks were picked up off the section we claimed.

It was in the fall of 1890 that we moved into our dugout, but 1891 was the first crop we made on our claim. We did not know what really would grow and had to plant and experiment, but we had our hogs, chickens, and cows so did not worry about the crop much. . . .

We did not need a great deal of money for everything was raised at home. Quail were so very plentiful that husband decided to take a load to Vernon to sell and killed a lot, and I dressed them just as nice, but he could not sell one. The next time he took them to sell, he took them just as he had shot them, feathers and all, and sold a lot at one dollar a dozen. We had thought they would spoil was the reason we dressed them at first, but they didn't. After that he often took a hundred or two birds whenever he would go to town. Eggs were five cents a dozen and sometimes I could get fifteen cents a pound for my butter.

We did not know if cotton would grow, but in 1897 we planted nine acres and got nine bales of cotton. We had to take it to Quanah to have it ginned. We got four cents a pound and I thought we were rich. I got several bolts of calico of fifty yards in a bolt and shoes for all the children. Flour, sugar, and coffee were the only groceries we had to buy all the time, and if we got out and had no money, husband would hitch up the team to the wagon and go out on the prairie and pick up enough bones to get what we wanted. He could get six dollars a ton for bones. . . and our wagon would hold half a ton, so we usually knew about what to expect. It would take all day to pick up a wagon load of dry buffalo or cow bones. . . .[8]

Over on Salt Fork of Red River there were all the wild plums and grapes you wanted. When we went to gather them, we took our dinner and stayed all day, usually bringing back a wagon load of which ever we went for, plums or grapes. We put them up various ways, but I think plum leather was the favorite way of saving the plums for winter use. You could use plum leather in so many ways, but pies were the best of all. I would let the plums stand until they were mush ripe and then work out the seed and spread the pulp out on a clean cloth and lay it in the sun to dry. When it was dry, you could roll it up and hang it up in sacks for use whenever you wanted it. [These were perhaps early "Fruit Roll Ups."] My cobbler pies became so famous that a carpenter out of Mangum met me about ten years ago and told me he would never forget those cobbler pies he had to eat at my house when he was helping to build the school house. (72:340, 342, 345)

Comanche, b. 1881

I like to go to Deyo Mission.[9] Its location is very convenient for most all the Indians of this county. On Thursdays the Indian women have quilting parties. (82:44)

Cherokee freedwoman, b. 1852

I am eighty-five years old, being born in slavery, near Tahlequah, Cherokee Nation, June, 1852. My father and mother belonged to D[—] R[—], who lived southeast of Tahlequah at a place called "Caney" and did his trading at Tahlequah. . . .

Mr. R[—] was a very old man and his sons did all the bossing of the slaves about the field work. We raised wheat, corn, and Hungarian Millet, and we gathered the blades off the corn and bound them in bundles for fodder, to take the place of hay as there was no wild hay growing near.

We had plenty to eat, good horses to ride, and plenty of good whiskey to drink. Our masters were kind to us here in the Indian country and there were no restrictions. . . .

The Landrum family was one family that believed in educating their slaves, and they taught them all to read and write, from the time they were children. This had a telling effect and many of the negroes returned after the war [Civil War], and went to work for their old masters. . . .

When I was ten years old, my master sold me to Col. William Penn Adair, a very famous Cherokee lawyer. . . . They just took me over there and left me, and I didn't know I had been sold for a long time afterward. D[—] R[—] had had a big lawsuit and employed Colonel Adair to defend him, and I was sold to pay the lawyer fee. (106:442, 444, 445)

Anglo, b. 12-21-1851 Platte County, Missouri

The next year good crops were raised. Our garden was very good. I remember we had lovely peas. One day I picked and shelled a pan full of peas and as we were going to town that afternoon, I took them with me and sold them for 25 cents. I was quite happy as this was the first money we had made on the claim. That very evening, just after we got home, a terrible hail storm swept through the country ruining our lovely garden and the wheat crop, too. However, sweet potatoes made a pretty good crop as did our tomato plants, and we had plenty of fine tomatoes.

I did all I could to make our house look nice. I remember how hard I worked papering the walls with old newspapers, and Mr. H[—] [her husband] was always reading something from the walls. (63:63)

Anglo from Indiana, b. 1855

There was quite a lot of wild game, but I could not fire a gun and as Mr. R[—] was always sick, we never had any meat unless a neighbor brought it to us. I had quite a few turkeys that I had brought with me, but men from Edmond would come to hunt, and thinking the turkeys were wild, they soon shot most of them.

It seemed that we were handicapped from the first. I had to sell our cows one by one to provide provisions. Our main food was cornbread and side meat. . . . (41:501)

Anglo, b. 1860

We planted corn, sweet potatoes, and beans and cultivated mostly by a home-made hoe. The hoe was made in this way. The men would go out and look for a tree that had a straight branch as long as a hoe handle, and they would cut the tree down and cut off about ten or twelve inches long where the limb was and split the log and hew it as thin as a hoe. They held it over the fireplace to dry, and then it was ready to be used. This kind of a hoe would last longer than the hoes we use in these days. (21:262–63)

Anglo from Indiana, b. 1864

They [interviewee and her husband] next built sheds for their stock, which sheds were built of poles for the sides with straw roofs. A chicken house with walls of sod and a straw roof was also built and a well was dug convenient to the house. They brought about ninety chickens, nine head of cattle, four horses, and four young hogs to butcher the following year. They had but $35.00 in money to run them that year or until they could grow another crop, but Mrs. H[—] being unusually strong, energetic and industrious, planned that by carefully using the milk from their cows to make butter, she could produce a surplus each week above the family needs which, with a surplus of eggs from the chickens, would almost pay for the groceries that it would be necessary to buy. They took wheat to a mill at Oxford, Kansas, a distance of about sixty miles and had it made into flour for their bread. They usually took enough to run them for several months. . . .

In the spring of 1897, they planted corn and castor beans most of which were on sod land, and this, in addition to their few acres of wheat all made a fair yield. Mrs. H[—] worked in the field to help shock wheat during harvest time; she helped stack hay, gather corn, or did anything that was to be done. In addition to the work out of doors she cared for her children, did her housework, family washing, etc. She churned the milk from their cows in a stone churn with a wooden churndash, made most of the family's wearing apparel, bed sheets, pillow cases, etc., and patched and mended all wearing apparel for the family. Her dresses were mostly of calico, for ordinary wear, ten yards of calico being required to make a dress in keeping with the style of those days, and the price paid for calico was from three and one-half cents to five cents per yard. . . .

In the spring and early summer of 1894, Mrs. H[—] had canned considerable quantities of vegetables and fruit which they brought to their new home in Oklahoma Territory and they ate these canned goods the following winter which reduced their living expenses considerably. She had also dried considerable fruit and green corn for winter use. . . .

There were no automobiles, no electric nor other kinds of refrigerators, no kind of power washing machines, no electric sweepers nor other kinds of electrical labor saving devices. The women used big iron kettles to boil the clothes on wash days and used home made soap and a washboard to rub the dirt out of their clothing. They used metal and glass lamps that burned kerosene to furnish light in their homes and in other places. . . .

The family bathroom was a dark corner in the house where the old wash tub could be placed to serve as a bathtub. . . . (29:279–82)

Choctaw, b. none given

Cotton was raised for the purpose of making clothing, stockings, and gloves. They [the family] had no gins, so every night it was the job of the children to take a double handful of cotton and separate the seed from the lint before they went to bed. While they did this the women would make thread on the spinning wheel. (15:410–11)

Anglo from Illinois, b. 9-8-1839

My son lived in a sod house, had to go to the Kiowa and to the mountains to get enough fuel to keep from freezing to death. Sometimes they had to burn corn and cottonseed. We had some real cold weather in the early times and it was a problem to keep enough wood to burn. We visited with our son for several months then we went back to Texas and sold part of our stock. We brought about thirty head of cattle and horses. We also brought our furniture and chickens.

. . .

We located on Elk Creek north of Sentinel. We lived in a sod house and in a tent until we could haul lumber from Vernon, Texas. It took about ten days or two weeks to make the trip. We dug a well just as soon as we could, but the water tasted just like copper and we could not drink it so we used it for a stock well. (113:140–41)

Cherokee, b. 1-23-1887 Vinita

There was hardly a house in the entire country, only a few Indian huts scattered far and wide. There was no land in cultivation so they [her parents] were truly pioneers, indeed, with high hopes and with hearts undaunted, with cherished dreams of the future, clearing the path ahead, they forged their way into the wilderness to build a home for themselves and their children. In 1882 my father, with only one old span of mules, hauled lumber from Spavinaw, a distance of about fifteen miles and built himself a new frame house, consisting of three rooms, one story high, and in 1896 added another story, with two additional rooms with a big fireplace at each end of the house. The old house is still standing and is one of the oldest land-marks in Craig County. My father died in 1900, and my mother March 1, 1930, but their works and memories live on.

. . .

I was married to Henry L. C[—] July 10, 1904. . . . I was so young, only seventeen years old and Henry was only twenty-one. We came back to my home and lived with my mother until we built our own home in 1905, a brick bungalow. We secured the brick to build our house from a very famous old brick mansion built by Johnson Thompson, for his son, Dr. Joe (or Jeter) Thompson, now of Tahlequah. The bricks were moulded and burned on the ground where the house stood before the Civil War, by negro slaves. It was a great two story colonial house, with a brick garage, called then a "gay-age", spoken like carriage. The smoke-house, servant quarters and kitchen were built away from the main house. . . .

This old brick mansion stood on the north bank of Grand River, less than a mile from where the $20,000,000 Grand River Dam will be built, across the river from the town of Disney.

There were two of these brick houses built by Johnson Thompson, one on the south bank, which will be 100 feet under water when the dam is completed and now belongs to the Hydro Electric Company of Tulsa. We bought the one on the north bank from H. Ward.

In April 1904, there was a terrible cyclone, the worst storm in the history of the Indian Territory. It traveled up Grand River, at twelve o'clock noon and almost took the country clean. . . .

But that is where we got our home, out of the storm. H. Ward's house was so badly damaged that he didn't think it would be worth while to rebuild it, so we bought the brick for a song, and immediately started to work tearing it down, cleaning the brick, having a wagonload each day, just we two with no one to help us.

My husband would get upon the wall and tear the bricks down with an old file blade and slide them down a trough and I would catch them and cut the mortar loose from them and stack them back. It took us all fall and winter to get the bricks ready to build our house and believe me, plenty of hard work and determination but that is what we built our house upon, for we had no money but we had good credit, which was built for us by our parents.

A. J. Thompson laid the brick for us and Tom Spradlin did the carpenter work. My husband told all the boys who would come and help cover the house that he would give them a house warming. It looked like blackbirds on our roof, and when they finished, on the 24th day of March, 1905, we moved in and I shall never forget that day. We had very little to move; mostly what our parents gave us. We loaded everything onto a hay frame, and my mother came with us. She took a Bible and a sack of meal into the house

first. She said we would always have a Christian home and plenty
to eat if we would do that. This was an Indian superstition but it
proved to be true in our case for thirty-three years to this date.
(100:116–17, 120–21)

THREE

Living with the Animals

In the eastern Oklahoma woodlands lived deer, bear, river buffalo, and the occasional elk, while on the vast western plains ranged buffalo and antelope. Throughout Oklahoma, mountain lions, wildcats, coyotes, wolves, and eagles preyed on both animals and people. The land supported snakes, turtles, lizards, and prairie dogs, and vast flocks of birds flew through the skies. The rivers were home to innumerable fish and freshwater clams, and in the swampy areas of rivers lurked alligators and gar.

When the people of the Five Tribes were removed to Indian Territory, some brought cattle, horses, and hogs. Many of the hogs wandered and lived wild in the woods. Added to these animals were cattle herds moving regularly through the territory to Kansas railheads in the years after the Civil War.

Women lived in a land teeming with these animals, birds, fish, and reptiles, and because frontier life was difficult they had to consider the creatures surrounding them in terms of survival. Women heard the haunting screams and cries of panthers and wolves echoing in the night, knew that hogs were omnivorous and ate whatever fell in their paths, and killed snakes competently. Even in the home, early settlers were plagued by tarantulas, centipedes, rattlesnakes, and fleas. Clearly, women on the Oklahoma frontier lived with animals in intimate relationship, engaging in daily routines of feeding and herding their stock, gathering eggs, and avoiding dangerous animals. To do such things required an intense awareness of the creatures and game upon which their survival and that of their families depended.

Anglo from Texas, b. 1881

There were not many animals near us. Wolves, possums, coons and squirrels. The doves were the most plentiful of the birds and they made the most lonesome sounds in the spring. I did not like to hear them. Crows gave us a good deal of trouble pulling up corn just after the corn came through the ground. Woodpeckers were always pecking on the logs of the house and would nearly drive one wild.

There were lots of snakes and I always killed every one I saw, but I do not think there were many poisonous snakes. I know there were no rattlesnakes in that part of the country. We watched the clouds a lot but never had a storm over there. (89:114)

Anglo, b. 1856

As to the wild things, we had plenty of wild antelope, wolves and deer. We could stand in our yard and see as many as eight or nine antelope in a bunch.

The rattlesnakes were to be dreaded for they were very poisonous and there were a great many of them. One time a child was sent out to get the turkeys in, and a rattlesnake bit him and he died right soon. There were no doctors closer than Quanah or Mangum. Mangum was forty miles away and Quanah was farther. (104:109)

Cherokee, b. 5-1-1877 Logtown, Arkansas

Mrs. W[—] and her daughter Nora became lost one evening. They had gone to hunt the cows in a place called Panther Hollow, so named because a panther made it his habitat. As it began to grow dark the two were unable to find their way home. They thought they heard Mr. W[—] calling them and started to follow the sound only to find it was the panther they had heard. Mr. W[—], who at the time was ill with pneumonia, became worried, and as the darkness increased, felt sure they must be lost. He got out of bed, loaded his gun, and fired both barrels simultaneously, thereby making such a loud report that the lost ones heard it and were able to find their way home again. (62:133–34)

Cherokee from Arkansas, b. 1877

There had been guests for dinner that day and, following the custom of the time, the children waited until after the elders had eaten to have their dinner. The children had barely seated themselves at the table, which was set out of doors, when the storm struck. The table was over-turned, breaking most of the dishes, while little Minnie was blown clear out of her chair. The tent was torn to shreds and the old high cupboard was tipped over but a cake sitting on the cupboard, which Mrs. W[—] had baked for her husband's lunches and had just removed from the oven, by one of those freaks of chance, fell to the ground undamaged. As it struck the ground a hog tearing around outside the tent saw the cake and sticking his snout into it got severely burned and with a loud squeal dashed away again. (62:132–33)

Anglo, b. 1855

We could stand in the door of our dugout and pick off an antelope most any morning with a Winchester. We could see them trotting along a dozen in a herd most any time of day. There were still a few deer over in the brakes on Salt Fork of Red River. We usually wanted a deer for Thanksgiving. We thought it better meat than antelope. There were wild turkeys, prairie chickens, and quail to eat any time we would trap them, for they came into the yard and ate with the chickens if there was snow on the ground and stayed around the feed stacks all the time.

Rattlesnakes, tarantulas, and centipedes kept me so frightened that I never dared let the little girls out of sight of the house for everyone went barefooted. Our neighbor, Mr. Hobbs' wife, sent her two little girls out to hunt a turkey nest and one was bitten by a rattler and died before morning. We seldom stirred from the house on any errand without having to stop and kill a rattlesnake. I have gotten off my horse, loosened my saddle girt and taken the saddle girt and beaten a snake to death a lot of times.

I was going with husband to a sale once and right by the road stood up a rattler on his tail. He was just behind a little mesquite bush. We stopped the team, took a trace chain, and beat him to death. Before we got him dead good, here came his mate and we had to kill another snake. Before we got away from that little glade I think husband had killed five as big rattlers as I ever saw. I was afraid to let the children go to the field. One spring the corn had almost gotten too hard to eat as roasting ears before I found time to go myself. I was walking down the row looking for the biggest, greenest ears when I kept hearing a rattle and there was a big old rattler going right down the row in front of me giving warning and just hurrying to get a chance to coil to strike at me. Tarantulas, centipedes, and spiders had to be shaken out of bed real often. We never dared crawl into bed without first shaking out all the covers and sheets to see what was hiding in them. They would come out on the ceiling of the dugout and drop on the table where we were eating or on our shoulders or laps—it was surely a scary time for us mothers and many people died from the bites and stings.

. . .

Big old dog fleas were a big nuisance. You could not keep them out of the dugouts. I have had my whole floor covered with these devil's claws trying to keep fleas off the bed. A devil claw is a kind of sticky plant that grows on the prairie that fleas like to get on and they claim once on a devil's claw a flea cannot get loose from the sticky substance that binds their legs to the plant.

. . .

We never knew when we went away from home just what we would find in the dugout when we got back. Once we found three snakes coiled up on the steps when we lifted the door. Another time we found a badger had dug his way into the front room and was living peacefully on the floor as though he thought it just another and bigger hole than he was used to. (72:340–42, 346, 348)

Cherokee, b. 1877

One time while still living along Bird Creek the four little girls ran off. Without telling their mother anything about it they started to follow their father who had gone to help a family of Indians do their butcherings something which Indians knew very little about. (This old Indian, incidentally, had two wives, one about his own age, the other a young woman, the two wives living quite peaceably together with the old man.) On the way to their father the little girls encountered a wild sow with eight little pigs. The sow started to attack the children, whereupon Nora, the oldest turned and ran away, but Etta, next oldest, putting Minnie and Lilly behind her fought the enraged animal until it finally turned and ran off. (62:135)

Anglo from Texas, b. 1857

We did not have many chickens or eggs for several years, not until the boys got a pack of hounds and killed the coyotes out. We did not miss the chickens so much for there were so many plover and quail. The boys made traps for them and we had them every day. Sometimes they would dress them and take them every day into town and sell them for five cents a piece. There was always plenty to eat and to spare. . . .

. . . I was so close to town that I kept boarders a lot. We early got a good pack of fox hounds and you could sell them if you wanted to, for running coyotes was a real sport for the young men.

. . . My son watched them [Indians] have a terrapin roast once. The Indians go around all over the prairie and gather terrapins up in gunny sacks; they make a big brush fire and empty the terrapins into the fire without killing them and stand around with sticks and punch them back into the fire if one runs out. When the shell pops open, the terrapins are raked out and eaten right in their hands out of the shells. (80:363–64, 366)

Cherokee from Arkansas, b. 1877

Into the [Tulsa] stockyards thousands of head of cattle were shipped yearly, usually in the spring, then released for western 3-D pastures. By the time they reached Tulsa many of the cattle were unfit to go any further. The cattlemen, instead of disposing of them, would leave them wherever they happened to fall to roam the town if they ever got up again. [There was] an old dugout into which they would frequently stray, then start to attack the children when they came to use the dugout. Sometimes the exhausted cattle would get into a ravine, be unable to get out again, and just die there creating a terrific stench. Then sometimes they were vicious enough to attack people, making it unsafe to have them about, a constant source of worry to mothers of little children. Many times they would be skinned for the hide and the carcass left to decay by the hundred, adding to the stench. . . .

Mr. W[—]'s [her husband] oxen were stubborn animals, not to say stupid. After one of his long logging trips, not only would Mr. W[—] be tired but the oxen would be also, as well as sulky. As soon as they reached home the oxen, still yoked together, would make a run for the pond which Mr. W[—] had dug about a quarter of a mile from his house and plunge in. One time one of them, an old "surly," would not come out again when Mr. W[—] wanted him to, so Mr. W[—] started to whip him. This made "old [Surly]" so angry that he stuck his head under the water and held it there until he drowned, and the other ox, still yoked to him, had to pull him out.

Old Lion was a mean animal with black keen horns, and so vicious that if left free for an instant he would attack anyone in sight. But he was a great worker, pulling the entire load if the other member of the team shirked. In fact he pulled himself to death. Mr. W[—] was driving a load on the West Third Street [in Tulsa] hill which at that time was much steeper than it is now. The load was a heavy one and the other ox began to shirk, leaving old Lion to pull the whole thing. Old Lion never gave up, but just looked back, whined, and pulled so hard that he burst something and died right there in his tracks. (62:171–74)

Anglo from Texas, b. 1888

Each Indian had his own hogs which they claimed had been tame ones when they were turned loose. Each Indian had his hogs marked by different cuts on their ears. I would call them wild hogs for they were vicious and would chase a person. My cousin sent my older brother out to kill a hog and showed him the one to kill. He ran after the hog and it ran under a house and he "took after" it when it came out on the other side and killed it. An old Indian saw him as the hog came out from under the house and ran after him hollering at him in the Creek language but he didn't know what was the matter and was very busy trying to kill the hog. He dragged it home and saw that the Indian was following him. My cousin went out to meet the Indian, gave him a plug of tobacco, and paid him $1.00 for the full grown hog. Brother had killed the Indian's hog instead of my cousin's. (94:388)

Anglo from Texas, b. 1869

There were lots of wild turkeys in the woods and Father would take his gun and go early in the morning and kill some for dinner. Gobblers usually make a noise about sunup; this would let my father know where they were and he would have no trouble in killing all he wanted, one or two, for our dinner. . . .

We had a trough at the well where the horses drank, and Father would sometimes go down to the well and watch the bees come there for water. He was very patient and would watch the bees leave. After getting some water, they would go straight to their tree or hiding place, and by following them, Father would locate the honey. We had a lot of this. . . . (100:408–409)

Cherokee, b. 1877

The Creek Indian method of fishing was by the use of the devil's shoestring. They usually fished in groups, each man bringing with him a small mallet, a bundle of roots of the weed known as devil's shoestring, and a hickory post four or five feet long and four or five inches in diameter, one end of which was sharpened into a point, the other end flat. Proceeding to a fairly deep creek they would select a deep hole, wade out into the water and drive their posts in a circle, a few inches of the post extending above the water. The roots of the weed would then be placed on top of the post and beaten until the juice ran out and washed down into the water. The sound produced by the beating was similar to that of the croaking of frogs in spring. After the beating had been carried on for some time the fish would begin to float to the top of the water, the men then shooting them with bow and arrow. If a fish dived, the man who had shot it would dive under after it.

While the fishing was in progress the women of the party kept a large kettle of lard hot on the bank of the river. As the fish were caught they were cleaned, rolled in corn meal, and cooked in the hot fat. Then they were eaten right there along the river, accompanied by sour bread and coffee.

At one time [they] were preparing for one of these fishing parties, when, just before they were ready to start, as Mrs. H[—] was removing some pies from her oven, an Indian boy rushed into the house exclaiming, "Hurry! Baby there! Nora he want you!" (To the Indian everyone, man or woman, was "he.") [She] hastened to Nora's about three quarters of a mile to find Nora herself attempting to get hot water to wash the baby. Just as Mrs. H[—] entered Nora started to fall toward the stove. Mrs. H[—] rescued her, laid her on the floor, and sent the boy for a midwife who lived nearby, doing what she could for Nora while they waited. The midwife arrived, took charge, and all went well, but through all the excitement and bustle Nora's husband sat out in the yard, never lifting a finger to assist, as unconcerned as if nothing was going on.

After the interruption the fishing trip proceeded as planned except that Nora was not one of the party. On this particular trip, which was to Euchee Creek, the men seined the river, catching several very fine channel catfish, one of which was close to six feet long and weighed ninety-five pounds. Two other fine ones aroused the envy of everyone. (62:158–60)

Anglo from Arkansas, b. 1860

[The dogs were trained not] to catch any other animal than the one indicated by their master, or to unduly tear the ears of the animal caught. A gentle pat on the head and a kind word of encouragement was appreciated reward for the performance of these grueling duties. It will thus be seen that the pioneers are indebted to an appreciable degree to their faithful dogs for the assistance rendered in providing for their wants. Cattle, horses, and hogs would often break the rail fences with which fields were universally fenced at that time, and if permitted to stay in the fields would quickly destroy the growing crops. The everwatchful Shep, Bull, Rover, Tige, or Fan would bound up and, with the speed of the wind, chase the animals out of the field, and woe to the animal which did not vacate the field in the shortest possible space of time after being detected by the dogs. So, the pioneer dogs are entitled to be remembered as a very material part of the life of those whose history and customs we are now attempting to portray. Without the dog, the boys could not have enjoyed that rare experience attendant on the treeing of a rabbit, smoking him out with a fire made from leaves, then, when suffocated by the rancid smoke, to have "Brother Rabbit" come tumbling down out of the tree in which he had taken refuge; the dogs, with every nerve strained with eagerness to catch the rabbit; sometimes burning their feet or nose in the fire and emitting a yelp of pain; then, when finally the rabbit is caught, to battle the dogs for possession of the rabbit. What boy of those bygone days who has not with his dogs traced a rabbit in a hollow tree trunk and with a long straight stick, brushed at the end, twisted the rabbit out of his hiding place amid the bounding, yelping, and eager dogs. Yes, we must give the faithful and helpful dog a place in writing the history of this part of Oklahoma. (4:188–89)

Anglo from Mississippi, b. 1883

We children picked blackberries. . . . We wanted to take some to Thomasville, but we were afraid of the wild hogs. There were two women who took turns going with us to sell our berries. They took berries to sell, too. We got the whole sum of fifteen cents a gallon for them.

We could hear the wild hogs with their teeth popping, and they roared like mad hogs. They made a horrible racket like stampeding cattle.

One of the women told me the story of how one of her cousins, a child, went to his aunt's house for something. He didn't come home so they went to hunt him. They found his hands and feet and a skeleton of him. The wild hogs had done their worst. We never saw the hogs though, but she wouldn't let us go in the forest alone. I believe I said it was three miles to Thomasville from our house. (41:490–91)

Anglo from Ohio, b. 1862

I have seen many wild turkeys in the Choctaw Nation. I have seen the wild ones come up to the neighborhood of your farm cabin home and, if you were raising tame turkeys, they would have great fights and many times I have had to go out in the edge of the woods and timber and separate my tame drove from the fighting of the wild drove of turkeys. . . . (63:268–69)

Anglo, b. none given

The coyotes were so thick they would come right up to the hack and smell around and the children were afraid to go to school for they would hardly get out of their way. The children would sometimes throw the coyotes food crumbs from their lunch baskets like you would a dog.

One followed one of the girls nearly to the house one afternoon and her father got his gun and went out and shot it. We tanned the hide and made a rug to put by her bed. I could go out and kill an antelope if we needed meat. There were abundant rabbits whose meat was as white as chickens, and of which we were very fond. We could twist one of them out of a hole in the ground where they would burrow anytime and since they were very destructive to fruit trees and gardens, we often hunted them when we did not really need them for food. We had a bird dog named Jim. Everything we would kill we would dress and cook and offer it to Jim. If Jim ate it, we would; if he wouldn't, we wouldn't. He would eat anything I ever prepared to eat except possum. I caught a possum in the hen coop, and dressed him. I let him lay all night in salt water and the next morning roasted him so nice and brown with sweet potatoes in the pan. It surely did look good to eat so I fixed Jim a plate of the possum, but Jim would not eat it, so neither did we. I never tried cooking another possum.

We always slept under the wagon if it was pleasant weather. One night the biggest coon I ever saw came nosing around. We got clubs and everything after him, and I finally got a shot at him and killed him. His pelt made a pretty neck piece after we tanned it. I was here all alone one afternoon when a badger came galloping up to help himself to a fowl. I hit him at the base of the head with a club, and laid him out. When the folks got home I had his hide already stretched on a board to dry, as a badger makes a pretty back for a chair.

One morning we were sitting at the table rather late when we heard hounds. We all came up to see what it was all about. It looked like a bunch of boys and dogs with a coyote cornered. Mr. H[—] [her husband] said, "I'll get my gun and go help." It turned out to be a bear. Mr. H[—] shot it and all the neighbors had bear meat to eat, for it was rare that a bear was seen in this country. One of the men made a rug from the pelt. . . .

Since the Indians are not here to eat the terrapins they are more than a nuisance. I have not been able to have a cantaloupe in several years for they eat them off the vine as soon as they come on. They are very destructive to a garden by eating peas, cucumbers, tomatoes, beans, and in fact most everything. Mr. H[—] used to go out every morning early with a tow sack and gather them up and bring them to the house and dump them into the cement tank where the horses drank and drown them for that is about the only way you can get rid of them. One day we caught one and cut an

"H" on his back and put him in the buggy and took him two or three miles west on our way to town to see if he would come back home. In two days we found him in the garden again. (29:251–54)

Cherokee, b. 1877

One time while picking berries they found a fawn. It was about the size of a lamb and spotted tan and white. Their mother wrapped it up in her apron and held its nose so it would not bleat, for if the mother doe had known they had her baby she would have trampled them to pieces. When their tent-home was blown away, little Lilly grabbed the fawn in one hand, a pet puppy in the other, and ran, but as she ran the terrific wind blew her over so that she fell upon the pet fawn, injuring it so severely that it died that night.

Another time the children went into the house to their lunch and when they returned to the playhouse, they found that a deer had dashed through it and upset all their pretties. (62:165)

Anglo from Mississippi, b. 1870

The canyons were named Booger Boo by the hunters who camped in there near the mouth of these canyons and were so named on account of the screams and cries of wild animals such as panthers, wolves, and others. These noises made by these animals could be heard three miles away by hunters who camped near the mouth of McGee Creek.

The reason the cries and screams of animals could be heard so plainly here was because of the way they were echoed back from the huge rocks and mountains. (82:22)

Anglo, b. 1855

My sister-in-law who lived about half mile away across the prairie had a very narrow escape from a panther. She had a nine months old baby and her husband went away before daylight on his way to Quanah. Later in the day she meant to come over to my house to stay the night for he would be gone all of two days and a night with good luck. She heard something scratching on the top of the dugout and began to wonder what it was. A little dog that they had would go near where the scratching was and bark, then tuck his tail between his legs and run under the bed as though very much frightened. My sister-in-law did not know what to do. She did not have a gun, for her husband had taken it with him. About the only thing she could do was to sit still and wait for daylight, which she did. She peeped out when it began to get light and said there was a panther scratching away at the top of the dugout. He looked to be twenty feet tall from his fore feet he was scratching with to the end of his tail. He got tired and went away, but not before he had gotten a big enough hole in the roof to look in. (72:338–39)

Anglo, b. none given

After disposing of his holdings, he [her father] came East to the Indian Territory proper and settled temporarily in the Choska bottoms across the river north of Haskell. His cattle had been raised on the Kansas prairie and knew nothing about acorns. When he went out one morning and found twelve of his fine cows dead from eating acorns, he thought it was time to move. It was quite a loss as he had refused $100.00 a head for the cows.

. . . Several cowboys would accompany him on the trips with their camping outfits, chuck wagons and trained dogs. A well trained dog could do the work of several men as they would go over and under the herd if they saw one straying from the line. As night came on the men would circle the herd and hold them in one spot until the cattle were settled for the night, always selecting an open space as cattle never slept in the timber. Two or three men would be detailed to keep watch during the night in case some nervous cow had insomnia and decided to take a walk.

The Ranch was enclosed with a three strand wire fence and as I had learned to ride when I was almost a baby, I began to help herd the cattle at the age of ten. When I was in my early teens, I began riding the "line" for my father. I rode eighty miles a day for many days at a time, forty miles around the line and forty miles back. To those who know nothing of horseback riding that seems incredible, but with a swiftly moving horse who traveled with such ease, it was no harder than sitting in a rocking chair. The object of these long rides was to inspect the fences to see that no cattle "rustlers" had pulled up the posts and flattened the fence and driven out unbranded stock during the night. The cattle business was at his height then. It was always an interesting time in the spring and fall when the different outfits started off with their chuck wagons and camping equipment. Always with the Shepard dogs trotting quietly until they were called into action when they displayed as it seemed real human intelligence. My early training and outdoor life had given me a strong body and a fearless mind. I learned to rope and throw a yearling as well as any man. I always wore high boots which my father had made to order. As the dogs were valuable, so were the cow ponies, so well trained that it seemed as though they were able to read a cow's mind. While she was thinking of breaking from the line, the pony had already sensed it and was ready to dart after her. If the rider was not alert, he would find himself sitting on the ground. (1:194–96)

Anglo, b. none given

We have our milling done at Blue. The neighbors took turns. Each Saturday was milling day, and one man would go and take all the neighbors' sacks of corn and wheat. The next Saturday another neighbor would go.

The country was all open and covered with cattle. I've seen as many as five hundred following the wagon as my husband returned from the mill. They would smell the meal and salt and were trying to get it. (80:102)

Anglo from Russia, b. 8-30-1884

Once I took Mr. and Mrs. Becker over to the agency to hold their meeting and on my way back, I got lost. I drove for miles and miles, in circles I suppose. Mr. Becker's big dog always followed the buggy; it was coming home with me as usual, but I never thought of the dog for a good while; when I noticed it, it was running ahead of me, then meeting me barking very loud, then the thought came to me to follow the dog. I let it lead the way and soon we were home safely. (26:150–51)

Cherokee, b. 1887

I was married to Henry Letton C[—], a Kentucky saddle horseman. I was always a great lover of horses and when my prince charming came along on a beautiful blue blooded saddle horse, I "gobbled" him. We were married July 10, 1904 by Reverend J. J. Carroll. We had eloped in a buggy and driven five miles to our pastor's home and were married as we sat in the buggy. (100:418)

Anglo, b. 1874 Bowie County, Texas

I could drive a team with the best of them. Once ten or twelve negroes had loaded a wagon with cotton and were trying to get it up the hill from the old run to the road up by our house. The load was heavy and their team was small and they had worried them till they had balked. The wheels were cut in the sand till it looked like no team could get it out. They came to the house for our team. My husband was not there, but I told them to harness the team and go on back down there, I'd be along in a moment. I got my bonnet and got down there. I told them that when my team pulled it up, they were not to let the wagon run back but to hold all the purchases we had. I got up there and spoke to that team and they walked out with that load. Those negroes looked at me so admiringly. They thought I was wonderful. (43:229–30)

Cherokee, b. 1877

Mr. W[—] [her husband] made the Run into old Oklahoma when it was opened to settlement in 1889. He succeeded in filing on a claim near Chandler, but it was not a very desirable one and W[—] never went back to it nor took any steps to prove it. He had ruined his best horse in the dash so that it was never any good from then on, and died not long after. (62:181)

Anglo from Ohio, b. 1862

One fourth of July, the first fourth after the country was opened, the Indians had a beef to kill here in El Reno; they almost tortured it to death shooting arrows into it. They had seemingly gone wild again. The law went to the camp and shot the poor thing and put it out of its misery. (63:271)

Cherokee, b. 1877

When living along Bird Creek, [the interviewee] had to come to Skiatook to do her trading, the trip, from near Avant, being made on horseback and taking the entire day. Wild animals sometimes had to be fought off. Mrs. W[—] sometimes found a mountain lion after her chickens. Hogs sometimes dragged to the barn with their entire hams eaten out or torn out by mountain lions. This was when the family was living along Euchee Creek, not very close to other settlers. Once, while living on North Boulder in Tulsa, Mrs. W[—] was in her garden gathering turnips when she was attacked by a huge bull snake. She beat if off with a hoe but was almost exhausted before she was able to hack it to pieces. When the snake reared up, it reached almost as high as her shoulders. (62:184)

Cherokee, b. 1887

We have produced some real fine show horses. In 1913 we had the best three-year-old saddle mare in the state, and won the $100 silver loving cup at Oklahoma City with her. Her name was Cherokee Rose, by Monarch. (100:443)

Cherokee, b. 1-23-1887

One time my brother, Robert, bought some peacocks. They were beautiful birds, with a tail spread of about seven feet. They roosted on the highest limb of a great tree in our yard. When he bought them, no one in our community had ever heard one yell. They screech out in the night, and sound like something screaming at a high pitch. All of our neighbors for miles around said they had heard a mountain lion. Everyone was afraid to go out after night and it was a long time before we found out it was our peacocks they had heard. So many tales got started about this mountain lion—someone had seen it, someone had seen where it had eaten a pig, or a calf, etc. It was real funny after they found out what the noise was. (100:426)

Anglo from Texas, b. 1872

I remember another time I was visiting my brother over in Greer County, eight miles from Granite, west of the Gyp hills. He lived in an old dugout, dug down in the ground and covered with dirt. Out in front was a brush arbor. We had been sitting out there in the evening in the cool and it became bedtime. He picked up his two small boys, carried them in the dugout, laid them on the bed, and when he laid them down he heard a rattlesnake sing. He told his wife to bring his gun and the lamp. He told the boys not to move, that there was a snake in the bed with them. He shot its head off and it was coiled up between the boys. He said that it took nerve to do it but his boys' lives depended on him. He said that he saw the snake just as he laid the babies down and thought once that he would grab its head, but then he knew if he missed it that it would get him. (89:136–37)

Cherokee, b. 1-23-1887 Vinita

The startled teamsters fled in wild confusion and the mule herds stampeded into the darkness, several hundred of them plunging wildly over the cliff and hurtling out into space, to crash with a sickening thud on the rocks below. Their screams of agony and fright created a strange and horrible bedlam in the night and the face of many a Southern soldier blanched in terror at the unearthly sound that accompanied the booming gun fire. (100:430–31)

FOUR

Facing Adversity

Women in Indian Territory and early Oklahoma faced adversity while living in harsh and unforgiving conditions; therefore, realities for them offered simple choices. The vast majority of these women came to the territory with their men, and they had children when they arrived or within a relatively short time thereafter. This was true for women who arrived on the Trail of Tears, for women of post–Civil War Indian Territory, and for women of the land run era.

After the Civil War, Indian Territory contained many women who had been widowed. Indeed, Carolyn Ross Johnston notes that "more than one-third of adult Cherokee women were widows at the close of the Civil War, and one-quarter of Cherokee children (1,200) were orphans."[1] Additionally, increasing uncertainty prevailed for the entire population as the years passed because of an influx of whites into the land; because of economic structures changed by the arrival of railroads; and because of a rise in lawlessness as cattle drives added to the general confusion of the changing landscape. Then in 1892–1893 the Great Plains experienced severe drought, and many people in the Twin Territories were seeking a new economic start. Competition was fierce, and a certain amount of chaos, including violence, ensued.[2]

Women used their skills to survive, and they gave up the habits, if they possessed them, of economically privileged women back East. While there were pockets of people with economically well-to-do backgrounds, most of the women would be considered working-class today. Out of economic necessity, many women took on jobs that men were ordinarily thought to do during the time period, for example, herding cattle. In many cases, women became entrepreneurs, taking the attendant risks. A few were salaried. Women networked and partnered with family members and friends, taking on the task of economic survival while continuing to care for homes and children. Economic competition brought corruption and violence, and women lived with constant anxiety.

Often women were left alone either temporarily when their husbands went on business trips or permanently when their husbands died. Many had to figure out how to continue on their own. The interviews, of course, express the experiences of those who stayed and won out.

To make it financially, the women assessed the needs of their communities and planned how to meet these needs, using skills gained in their domestic roles. They opened and managed stores alone or with husbands, wove cloth, laundered clothes, and rode out across Oklahoma prairies with partners on trading expeditions, competing economically in a country of sharp dealing.

In addition to lawlessness, women and their families were in constant danger from snakes and other dangerous creatures. Prairie fires could start suddenly and overcome an area in a short time. Hot winds destroyed major crop fields, leaving families without such basic foods as corn and wheat. A simple cold could develop into pneumonia, sometimes resulting in permanent weakness or death. Childbirth was always risky, as doctors were far away from the homes or were simply unavailable.

The Indian Pioneer Paper interviews with women reveal that Oklahoma's mothers were creative, skillful, and "tough as a boot." They proved a force to reckon with and contributed significantly to the economic base of the area. To do this they acted assertively in public spaces and in competition with men, rejecting stereotypes of the nineteenth-century woman.

Anglo from Texas, b. 1872

We made so many trips to Indian country and back to Texas I hardly knew which state was home until we bought out a claim five miles south and one mile east of Lawton.

We bought out a man's improvements for two hundred dollars. The claim was supposed to have a two room house on it, a good well of water and some fencing. We moved from the eastern part of the state in two wagons and a Spaulding hack; each vehicle had two horses hitched to it and we had two young fillies following.

When we got to our purchased property the first thing we noticed was that there were a lot of wagon tracks around the well and we asked why. The man told us that he had been letting the neighbors haul water. On drawing the water from the well we found that the water in the well was very muddy and shallow and it developed that the well was really a dry hole and they had hauled water and thrown into the well to fill the contract for we had bought a well of water with the land.

The land looked very poor and rough but my husband said not to mind that he had intended to move the house farther up on a hill and build it and then he would dig me a good well, which he did. He also said, "You just wait and see, I will make this place look so nice by the time we are ready to sell that some one will give me a good price for it." And after staying on that place for five years we did sell for $3,500.00.

We moved that two room house upon the hill and built three rooms on to it. We put out a nice orchard of plums, peaches, apples, apricots, most any fruit you could mention and they all did well; but the ones named did best of all. We set out a vine-yard which also did well. We planted peanuts every year and sold a lot. We did not plant much cotton or wheat but raised enough corn to fatten a lot of hogs for we sold hogs. We always had a lot of cured meat and I just loved to make my own soap. When we sold out there we came south of Altus and bought 180 acres which I still own. We had to live in a dugout here for several years and still have a half-dugout on the place. We always pick a sandy mixed soil for we think that grows everything better. We lived here twenty years; planted another orchard, fenced, cross-fenced and made us a beautiful country home. Some of our children had married and some needed to be in high school, so my man came to town and bought up a lot of lots in this part and began to build small houses to rent. He also built this cement block one for us to live in; we rented the farm.

. . .

We had hogs, chickens, calves, colts to sell all the time; not many, but enough for each when needed. We also had sweet potatoes, peanuts, corn and oats to sell, so we never wanted for anything. My children were always healthy and fine so life has been good. (89:50–52)

Anglo, b. 9-9-1877 Fredrickburg [sic], Texas

With our coming the whole clan was up in this country. Grandfather, Grandmother, uncles, aunts and cousins all whom the Civil War and Indians had left. Grandmother learned to be a midwife after the Civil War for she had never learned to do any- thing in her life but look pretty, and she felt that she must be useful now since the family was poor and had no slaves. She would go a hundred miles or more to deliver a child and I never knew her to lose a baby or mother during the twenty years of her active work. She delivered hundreds of babies and never charged a cent. Of course she was often given handsome presents and sometimes money.

Mother learned to be a seamstress. She cut by chart and made men's clothes the same as she did women's and children's. She has turned out as pretty coats, vests and pants as I ever saw a tailor make in my life.

With our family there came two boys and two girls so we were a company of ourselves. We all rode anything you could put a bridle on in the way of a horse. We girls were never allowed to ride astride but had our side saddles and riding skirts and we could jump ditches or fences, swim a creek and herd a bunch of cattle with any boy. A neighbor said once that he thought we must have all been born in a saddle we could ride so well.

I was now about fifteen years old and only weighed eighty pounds but how I could ride and how I loved to ride. I was always guarding the cattle, keeping them out of quicksand or driving them to water. I have herded more than one bunch of cattle here where this town of Altus is built and while the cattle grazed no one could see me or my horse without coming right up onto me as the grass was so very high. (89:66–67)

Anglo from North Carolina, b. 2-21-1868

My husband and I settled five miles west and one mile north of Altus. We filed on a quarter section, and as soon as we were able, bought another quarter. A few years ago one quarter of this land brought $15,500.00. The other brought over $17,000.00.

The first few years were very hard indeed, principally because we had no start. We did not even have sufficient clothing. If some of the neighbors had not helped us, I don't know what we would have done. They helped us in many ways, even to loaning us cows to milk.

We got our supplies from Vernon, Texas. It took some three days to make the trip. My husband sometimes hauled merchandise for the Hightower Grocery at Altus. On one of these trips his wagon was overturned by a head rise in the river, and all his merchandise got wet. He had several hundred pounds of flour on the load.

I suppose our lives were similar in all respects to those of other pioneers. We lived in a dugout, as did many others. We made every effort to get ahead, and we succeeded.

The town of Altus was very small when we first came to this country. There were only about twelve houses here, and the first court was held in a dugout. At one time lots were offered free to those who would fence them with wire, but most people were too poor to do this. From where we lived we could see only nine lights shining from dugout doors. Our first cotton crop yielded us four-teen bales. We received four cents a pound for it at Vernon, Texas.

After eleven years of successful farming, we moved to Altus and have lived here every since. Mr. A[—] died about three years ago.

Well, our pioneer days were frought [*sic*] with danger and hardships, but we won out and got our start in life. (12:538, 539, 541)

American Indian from Missouri, b. 1852

December 29, 1889 we removed to the Indian Territory and settled in Bartlesville. That was a hard winter for us, for the country was strange and conveniences few. My husband was herding cattle in the Osage and was away from home most of the time. We had a large family so I looked around for a way in which I might help with the expenses. My mother was a weaver and I had helped her when I was a child and until I was married. I had become a good weaver and weaving was in demand in the new country. There was a lady here who wove for $.10 a yard and charged extra for putting the work in the loom. I could see there was money to be made in this work and decided if I could secure a loom I would try my luck. This lady knew I could weave and was suspicious of me. Mr. Slade, a carpenter who lived near me, was handy about making furniture and small articles. One day I asked him if he could make a loom and he said he could if he had a pattern. I made him a pattern of corn stocks about 6 inches square and he decided if he had the dimensions he could take the pattern and build one. He knew this lady and made her a visit in regard to some work she had for him. While he was there he became interested in the weaving and while she was out of the room for a few minutes, he took the dimensions of the loom. I bought the lumber from the Overlee's Lumber yard and he built the loom for me, and ordered the slay from Kansas City.

I told some of my friends of my plans and asked them about their weaving; this soon advertised for me and I had more than I could do. I did not charge for setting up the work as the other lady did and did my work at the same price. I was making a good income when I was stricken with rheumatism and Dr. Bruce, our family physician, told me I would have to give up weaving. This was quite a blow and at first I would not listen to this warning and continued my work, until Dr. Bruce who was a rough spoken man, told me if I did not stop work, he would take the loom out in the yard and chop it into fire wood.

My son, Howard, had helped with the work and had learned to weave. He decided with my supervision he could do the work, so he raised the price to $.15 per yard and still had more than he could do.

I had bought a lot at 724 Shawnee in Bartlesville, mortgaged it to the Overlee Lumber Company for lumber to build a house. After this lot was paid for, I bought another and in the same way improved it. With Howard's help we built a home for each of the children. We all worked and soon had our homes and enough income to live comfortable. I now live in one of the homes we bought in the early days at 111 South Seminole. While I have not acquired a fortune of the worldly goods, I have enough to live comfortable my remaining years. My husband passed on two years ago and my daughter makes her home with me. (37:282–85)

Anglo, b. 10-16-1856 Indianapolis, Indiana

We worked a hundred acres of that place [the old fort near Doaksville in southeastern Oklahoma] that year [1884]. We worked lots of negroes, I have written before how superstitious the negroes were. When we would have them eat at my house so as to save time, rather than have them go to their homes when we're very busy, those negroes would never eat much, they were so anxious to get out of that house, which was said to be haunted.

After a year at the old fort, we built a double log house at Doaksville. It was a good one of hewn logs, and we lived in it about fifteen years, until we built our home and established a store and post office at Corinna, in Pushmataha County where we ranched for twenty-five years.

We traded with full-blood Indians. We bought their snake root, hides, etc., and in turn, sold them dry goods and groceries. We entertained them at our home, which was all very well until one old Choctaw Indian decided that he wanted to swap wives with Barney, whether we women liked it or not. Barney almost had to kill that Indian before he could convince him that neither he nor I wanted to swap. . . .

In the fifteen years that we lived in Doaksville we owned different stores and had different partners.

Once, Barney and John D. Wilson were partners in a store. It had not been so very many years since the "Wilson War" on Clear Creek at the water mill, when the full blood Choctaw Indians had run old John Wilson and his sons, John D., Willie, Edward H. and Rafe Wilson, all away over into Texas.[1] John Wilson was wounded in that battle. He carried the bullet in his knee to his grave. (38:120–22)

Anglo from Illinois, b. 1861

Those first years we raised good crops and we would market our surplus either at Pawnee or to the Osage Indians across the river. When we went to Pawnee Mrs. Carmean, my nearest neighbor, and I would strike out very early in the morning across the prairie in the general direction of Pawnee for there was no road. I wouldn't ever go by myself for I was afraid I would get lost. I would always let Mrs. Carmean drive the ponies and if anything broke or went wrong, she always seemed to know just what to do. When we took our produce across the river to the Indian camp, we always took one of the men with us for we were afraid of the Indians although they never offered to harm us. They seldom had any money but traded us calico, moccasins and Indian bead work. (37:129–30)

Anglo, b. 4-15-1855 Beanblossom, Brown County, Indiana

I had my own loom and made carpets and rugs for a great many people. In nine months I wove one thousand yards of carpet. I received one hundred dollars for my labor.

Six weeks out of every year we made sorghum and kept most of the citizens of Edmond supplied. We lived there for twenty-eight years and then sold out and moved to Edmond. (41:502)

Cherokee from Tennessee, b. 1864

In May, 1885, I was married to James Madison A[—], a white man, at Chattanooga, Tennessee. In 1892 my husband came out to the Territory in the vicinity of Vinita. He looked about and decided he would select a place near Vinita. He returned East, and in 1893 we all came out. Back East, at Chattanooga, we were married according to the laws of the land, but upon reaching Vinita, in 1893, we were again married, this time in accordance with the Cherokee laws. This was thought best in that my husband was a white man and I an Indian woman. In doing this, he became a member of the tribe and on equal footing with the other members. (12:426)

African American freedwoman, b. 1-18-1870
Father-Irish/Indian, Mother-Negro

I was born at Trenton, Kentucky and grew up on a tobacco farm. The Mammoth Cave is partly on this farm. We children loved to play there, but nobody else paid any attention to it. After while people began to come out from Nashville and Clarksville, Tennessee to see it. They would come on Friday and bring food and stay over Sunday to look at the cave.

There were no schools, but sometimes the Boss-man would have a teacher come and the children would be taught wherever it was handy. If the Mistress's house had just been cleaned up and she didn't want to be bothered with the school, it would be held in one of the houses of the colored people. I never saw a real school till I got to Kansas.

I went to Kansas City and later to Newton, Kansas. Lived there about five years just before Oklahoma was opened. People in Newton talked a lot about coming to Oklahoma, and when they came I came with them on the same train. Indians used to come to Newton and bargain with white men to guide them to good land when the country opened. I used to see them talking together on the streets. Then in the "Run" an Indian would grab the hand of the white man who had paid him and they would ride off fast as they could go towards the land the Indian had settled.[2]

There were a lot of houses shipped in flat, on flat cars. We called them "hooked up" houses because it didn't take very long to put up the sides and fasten them together.

I paid 50 cents for a lot on West Mansur and built me a house out of old barrels. It was a kind of pen with a roof of brush and a quilt over the brush. I dug a hole in the ground for my stove and began to take in washings. I burned grass and buffalo chips to heat the water.[3] There were lots of buffalo chips here. I had to buy the water from a man who hauled it from the Cottonwood. That river was bank full, and as red as blood. Most people did not know how to wash in such water, so I got plenty of washings to do. I charged 25 cents each for washing men's shirts, and that didn't mean ironing them either.

This is the way I cleared that red water: At night I made a big ball of stiff dough just out of flour and water and put it into the barrel of muddy water. In the morning all the red mud would be sticking onto that dough ball, and I could pour off the clear water.

. . .

Then I bought two lots across the street from Cassidy's on Mansur and built me a two-room house. I later sold it to Cassidys. (89:334–36)

Anglo from New York, b. 1850

I married early but my husband only lived a little while so when they were building Altus [in the years following the Unassigned Lands opening April 22, 1889] I came over and went to running a hotel. You gave room and board for $5.00 a week. I could buy three dozen eggs for 25 cents, large frying chicken for 15 cents and butter for 15 cents per pound. Sweet milk cost 10 cents a gallon and buttermilk 5 cents a gallon. I gave a dandy meal for 25 cents. When they put up the first steam laundry here I could get my laundry done for 1 cent a piece, sheets, towels and all and they were mangled too as all the flat work was. (89:75)

Cherokee, b. 1877

She [interviewee] was at home alone with her baby when, hearing a noise outside, she opened the door to see, as she said, "the biggest, ugliest, meanest-looking Osage I had ever seen." The man's head was painted, his ears were split and hung with keys, while he wore nothing but a breech-clout. He was seated on a paint horse whose head was practically inside the door when she opened it. He could speak no English, but, holding up a dime he pointed to a pile of sweet potatoes lying near the door. Still terrified [she] ran for John who was working a good half mile from the house. He returned with her and the sale of sweet potatoes was completed just as several wagons came rattling by, filled with Osages; the women who were seated on the floor of the wagons being bounced about in most amusing fashion. As the wagons passed, the man who was at the door whirled his horse and followed them. Soon he came galloping back again, rode to the door, pounded his sack of potatoes, and said something which [she] could not understand. By this time the wagons, too, came hurtling back and Mrs. H[—] began to think someone must be mad or crazy. It happened that one or two of the young boys in the party could speak a little English. They were able to make her understand that the man was neither mad nor crazy but merely wanted to buy more sweet potatoes. Since the H[—]s had a dugout full of them for sale, they were glad to oblige, but, instead of offering more money as pay, the women jumped out of the wagons and opened the bundles which they were carrying. The bundles contained calico which had been issued the Osages by the Government. Calico was soon exchanged for sweet potatoes and the Osages left the H[—]s in peace, while the little H[—] children wore dresses of Government calico for many a day. (62:162–63)

Anglo, b. 1861 Putnam County, Missouri

My husband was accidentally killed the second year we were on the claim, but I continued the farming with cotton as the main crop. One year I picked 8000 pounds—5200 of my crop—and 2800 pounds for others and got 75 cents per cwt for picking—and boarded myself.[4] By so doing I supported my four children and paid for my sewing machine. I would do my laundry and sewing at night.

To market the cotton I hauled it [from Blackburn] to Pawnee and sometimes to Perry—the trip to Perry could not be made in one day so I camped at Morrison or Lela.

At Morrison there were two stores and the owner of one of them had a feed store and he also had charge of the camping yard which was run by Mr. and Mrs. Morrison for whom the town was named.

I received $1.40 and $1.50 per cwt for the cotton at the market.

I often traded onions, sweet potatoes, or other produce to the Indians for pieces of calico and other articles that I could use for clothing.

On one occasion my brother bought a hog from an Indian and I was with him and when we were fording the river, two Indians on horseback met us and tried to force us to return the hog—but after a heated argument they went on and never bothered us anymore.

In 1899, I secured work as a cook for a threshing crew—receiving $1.25 per day. I returned to my claim in the fall and picked my cotton—after which I relinquished my rights to my land and was married to Mr. A[—] in 1900. We moved to Grant County in 1900 and in 1910 moved to Noble County. (12:392–93)

Anglo, b. 7-20-1872 Cass County, Texas

He [interviewee's husband] hauled groceries for the store from Ardmore. It took two days to make the trip and my husband was always gone one night. I was desperately afraid of the Indians and I hardly slept during the nights when my husband was away. I had heard of such terrible things the Indians had done, but I later found out that I had no need to fear them. They were as civilized in the Chickasaw Nation as I. They had peculiar ways of doing things, but our methods of living were as queer to them as theirs were to us. One thing I remember was that a Chickasaw always left a green switch at his door when he left home to signify that he was gone.

My children had heard such terrible tales about the Indians that they [had once] thought of them as being wild monsters. One day my children were playing with my small sisters on a creek near Father's place. My sister heard some men coming down the creek. When she looked up and saw Indians riding toward them, she began to run, saying, "The Indians are coming. Let's go to the house." One of my children looked at the approaching Indians and said, "Why, that's just men."

My husband put a small stock of groceries in one room of our log house. . . .

Our business became so good that my husband moved our store to Troy. This was the first store there. It was in a log house. My husband had groceries and dry goods, and when he got things on hand which he couldn't sell, he peddled them among the neighbors. Not long after he established the store, there was a mail line put through to old Mill Creek, and my husband blazed the road. He made two trips a week on a horse. It was on one of these trips that he became suddenly ill and didn't live to get home. He died at the home of a settler between Troy and Old Mill Creek. This left me alone with five girls.

My husband's partner in the store and my oldest girl took care of the store. Our herd of cattle had increased to eighty. My husband had taken several head of cattle on debts at the store. It was my task to ride after the cattle. We continued to pay our $5.00 permit each year.[5] The first summer after my husband's death, my youngest daughter had typhoid fever.

I had to stay very close to her bedside and couldn't watch my cattle. While she was sick, somebody stole ten of my finest heifers. That was all that was ever stolen from me though. Each fall I bought enough flour to do a year and stored it on a small platform fastened to the joists.

We never locked the doors when leaving home, and nobody ever entered our house while we were away or if anyone did, there was not anything missing.

I had a very difficult time making a living for my family of girls. I rented the land each year to a tenant, and we tried to keep

our part of the store going. Eggs were almost unsalable [*sic*]. Everybody had eggs and stores would hardly buy them, even at 4 cents
a dozen. (113:397–99)

Anglo, b. none given

There was work then, though; a man could get 50 cents a day
for splitting rails and 50 cents went a lot farther then. I remember
that mother sent a dollar to town by one of our neighbors for some
groceries. She got a fifty-pound sack of flour, a bucket of sorghum,
a gallon of coal oil, a box of matches, and some change back.

While we were living there Father drove some cattle from
Arkansas to Checotah, in the Territory; he was working for a man
named Coon Ratteree. The cattle forded the Poteau River close
enough to our house on the hill above Turtle Lake.

There was a post office at Enterprise and some general stores,
a blacksmith shop and a gin. The people around there were mostly
farmers, with a few scattered cattlemen here and there. Donahue
owned a store and so did a family named Robinson. There were
churches in Enterprise: Methodist, Baptist and Church of Christ.
(89:26, 28)

Anglo from Tennessee, b. 1890

I guess there were hundreds of tents. There were restaurants in
tents, rooming houses in tents, or so they called them. They were
simply cots put up in tents and rented out, mainly to workers on the
new railroad that was being surveyed for and the dump being built
for it. . . . The barber shops and stores were in tents. (89:98–99)

Anglo from Missouri, b. 12-21-1851

Laurine [interviewee's daughter] grew up and worked with us.
She helped me carry water for the plants, ran after the cows when
they got out and helped fix the fence to keep the cows from getting
out. Mr. H[—]'s [her husband] cousin told her she should have been
a boy; she was always doing boy's work. . . .

. . . While we lived in Marshall, Mr. H[—] was taken sick and died. I lived on in Marshall for awhile, then came to Guthrie in 1923. (63:259, 262)

Anglo from Texas, b. 8-20-1866

I made extra money nursing after we came up here. I have been a practical nurse since I was fourteen years old. There was much sickness in the early days. The settlers had what the doctors called "grippe." Today we call this the "flu." (92:234)

Chickasaw-Cherokee, b. 4-3-1837

My mother would go her neighbors and wash for them. I used to go with her and at one place the children all had sore eyes. They had two springs they used water from, one for drinking and other for washing. I was so afraid the children washed in the spring that we were supposed to drink from that I went down into the pasture and dug a spring and when it settled, I would lie down on my stomach and drink from it.

At one place where Mother went to wash, they had an upstairs to their log house and we stayed all night and I slept upstairs; I didn't sleep, I was so afraid. That was the first and last time I ever slept upstairs.

. . .

When we were first married Father gave us a small piece of bacon and said, "Now, you build to that." We never worried about meat as there was plenty of wild game; sometimes my husband would kill two deer a day and call me to help him bring them in. Some deer had such big horns that he would have to cut them off before we could drag the deer through the timber. Mr. A[—] would dress the deer and take it to Caddo and sell what we didn't need and on many mornings he has killed eight turkeys before breakfast. He would sell them dressed for a dollar and sometimes less. (12:172–73)

Anglo from Iowa, b. 4-5-1872

My husband had a friend who had married a Chickasaw woman and he controlled lots of good farming land and we were heading for his place [in approximately 1891]. The man's name was Jim Campbell, and he lived eight miles southeast of Mineo. Mr. Campbell had about four sections of land broken in a square. He had ten or twelve renters, who farmed it on shares. My husband rented and farmed one hundred acres of land there. He made about forty bushels of corn to the acre and sold his part to Mr. Campbell for twenty-five cents per bushel.

We bought our supplies and got our mail at Mineo.

. . .

I consider crab grass as being the growth which was most detrimental to farming in the early days. We were not bothered with insects, and there were very few weeds. (12:463–64)

Choctaw freedwoman, b. about 1857

It was at a big school "turn out" [at Spencer Academy, a Choctaw boarding school for boys] that my old master and mistress came to that I got acquainted with them again and went back to work for them. My old master's name was Mr. Sampson Folsom and my old mistress's—his wife's name was Mrs. Kitty Folsom. I called her "Miss Kitty." I would work in the field and in the house and would do just anything they had for me to do. They were Choctaw Indians. My parents were their slaves when I was born. After I went to live with Mr. and Mrs. Folsom we would sometimes go to Sunday School over at Pine Ridge Academy. The Reverend Mr. Cyrus Kingsbury was there then.[6] The last time I heard of him, he was living with a daughter-in-law, Maria Kingsbury. I guess they are all dead now.

I don't know what became of them.

Once, Miss Kitty took me to Paris, Texas with her, and the road went right past Rose Hill Farm. Mrs. Bailey was living there and was Miss Kitty's friend and we spent a night there. Mrs. Bailey had been the second Mrs. Robert N. Jones. She was a white woman. We went on across Horse Prairie, and crossed the river at a ferry. A man by the name of Wilkins was running that ferry then. They told me that all of that Horse Prairie used to be one big farm. I sure was glad to see that old place again for that was the first time I had been there since I was very small. After my daddy died, Mamma moved up to a place called Douglas where she died and is buried. It is now called Virgil.

. . .

Miss Kitty was a Colbert, my mother belonged to her folks. Mamma was Sukey Colbert; my father belonged to the Folsoms and was named Jarret Jackson. I ain't never been married. I'm a Jackson. Miss Kitty and Mr. Sampson Folsom were each about one half Choctaw Indian. (31:47–50)

Anglo from Kentucky, b. 1856

My father lived in Whitney County, Kentucky. We moved from there to Franklin County, Arkansas, then to Montague County, Texas and to Hollis in 1895. We are still living in Hollis.

We left Montague County in wagons. We had six children, two wagons, and two pair of good mules, five cows and some loose stock. We also brought some chickens, and our furniture but it wasn't much. We came to Quanah, Texas and forded the Red River for there were no bridges, and then we traveled on and on down the trail for that was all the road we had. . . . After an all day's drive we arrived at the place that was to be our home, which is two miles north of what is the town of Hollis now. . . .

Quanah, Texas was the place where we got our supplies. We would gather up a load of buffalo bones and take it with us to trade for supplies such as flour bought by the barrel, sugar, coffee, and clothing. I would go once a year to get clothing and I well remember getting at one time, one whole bolt of brown domestic which cost three cents a yard and calico at two and one-half cents, and I got some real nice calico for five cents to be used for our best dresses. Now those bones which we took brought eight dollars a ton. It took us three days to make the trip. (104:107, 109)

Cherokee from Georgia, b. 1849

If a white man wanted to work in the Territory, he had to, or his employer had to, secure a permit and pay $12.00 a year to permit him to work; finally the fee got down to $6.00 a year and then it cost nothing. There was plenty of graft with these permits on both the white and Indian side. (1:299)

Anglo, b. 1886 Chickasaw Nation, Indian Territory, parents from Kentucky

In the fall of 1899, we had raised a fine crop, had our cribs full of corn and one night when my father was away from home, my two brothers, mother and myself were getting ready for bed when we heard a noise out by the barn and by the time we got outside the barn and corn cribs were on fire; we worked hard trying to put out the fire, but could not stop it so we lost everything except our teams and wagon and household things.

Some men had been wanting the lease where we lived and they got it for soon after the fire we moved.

A few years later the men admitted burning us out and said they were at the edge of the timber watching us carry water trying to put out the fire.

There were several outlaws hung at one time between Ada and old Center. I do not remember the date of this hanging. (12:405–406)

Delaware, b. none given

My father and brothers were prosperous farmers and they operated on a large scale. The land was exceptionally good and the corn and wheat crops were abundant. Corn sold for 15 cents per bushel. We also raised hogs, cattle, and horses. Our water supply was obtained from the little creek on our farm, Whiteturkey Creek. We used this water for drinking purposes and it was very cold.

Our dining table was a long, homemade table and reached across the end of the room and we used tin cups and places. We had chinaware but seldom ever used it.

The closest trading post was Baxter Springs, Kansas, and it would take a week to make a trip for supplies. In 1857 Jacob Bartles came to the Indian Territory and established a saw mill at Yellow Leaf Ford on the Verdigris River. Later he established a general store on the banks of the Turkey Creek, then moved to Silver Lake a few years later when he saw Nelson Carr trying to establish a flour mill in the bend of the Caney River, where to get power it was only necessary to build a dam across and cut a sluice-way across the short neck of the bend, he realized this was a favorable location for a town site. He established a store and flour mill and later a blacksmith shop on this location and this was our first real trading post.

. . .

Our clothes were all hand-made and the women and girls' dresses were made to fit tight in the waist with skirts gathered full. The Indians had lots of money, because they had no place to spend it. We paid $10.00 a hundred for flour and $6.00 a hundred for meal. (2:471–72)

Miami, b. 1877

We have lived here at the agency for at least thirty-five years. Then there were lots and lots of nice homes here. It was a sort of camping ground for the Indians, too. They would come here and camp back down the creek, and many would stay here for months at a time. A lot of business went on here. There was a store up here close with a well behind it. It must have been across the road, because there isn't any well or remains of a well on this side. The Indians went there to get water a lot. The Indians traded at the store, and used mostly money for their buying. And they traded things like buffalo hides and buckskin, too, for groceries and clothes.

Pete West ran the store, and he lived up there where those cedar trees are (about a quarter of a mile from the agency, and back from the road about two hundred yards on the south side of the road.)

I remember when they moved the agency from here to Shawnee. Things began to die down right away, and in several years

Early Oklahomans share a picnic lunch, ca. 1918. The split-rail fence kept livestock out of the yard. The woman on the left is Mary Semple Hotchkin (b. 1837, d. 1917). The woman seated on the right is possibly Mrs. Pitchlynn. Courtesy of the Western History Collections, University of Oklahoma Libraries.

Creek women making sofka. Notice that they are wearing Anglo-style clothing as they pound corn in the traditional manner. Courtesy of the Western History Collections, University of Oklahoma Libraries.

Holding down a Town Lot in Guthrie Ok.

This pregnant woman makes herself at home on her lot in Guthrie, ca. 1889. The house is a combination of boards, a blanket serves as a door, and laundry is hanging to dry. Courtesy of the Western History Collections, University of Oklahoma Libraries.

Mansion in Oklahoma.

This black family in Guthrie, ca. 1889, used a combination of available materials to build their home: the land, poles, and canvas. Courtesy of the Western History Collections, University of Oklahoma Libraries.

This family poses in front of their Oklahoma dugout. Their clothing, live-stock, buggies, and domestic containers indicate that they are prosper-ous. Courtesy of the Western History Collections, University of Oklahoma Libraries.

Dora and Arthur Arvine Pittman pose in front of their sod home. It clearly shows the architectural ingenuity of pioneers in areas with little or no access to timber. Courtesy of Bill Pittman.

No stranger to hard work, this woman handles a wooden wheelbarrow to collect "cow chips," the available fuel for heating. Courtesy of the Western History Collections, University of Oklahoma Libraries.

117

In a railroad car used as the Dawes Commission office, Choctaws and Chickasaws register for land allotments, ca. 1900. Courtesy of the Western History Collections, University of Oklahoma Libraries.

On Closing Day 1912, Choctaw freedwomen and freedmen pose at the Oak Hill Industrial Academy, a Presbyterian mission school, in Valliant, McCurtain County.

Lena (*standing*) and her daughter, Beatrice (*sitting*), in the 1930s.

most of the houses had been taken down. We lived in quite a few of these houses around here, and have been at the house where we are now for about five years. There's a spring—two springs—north of our house up that creek about a quarter of a mile. They never run dry, and the Indians used to use those for their water supply. (4:79)

Anglo from Illinois, b. 1864

Some of the bachelor farmers in the neighborhood had raised a good crop of sweet potatoes, peanuts, and pop corn and having much more than they could use, they supplied Mr. and Mrs. H[—] with a liberal quantity, free of any charge. . . .

. . . Mrs. H[—] had a neighbor whose house caught on fire on one occasion from a kerosene lamp that had no globe on it as two little boys were fixing to retire at night; the house burned down and burned the two little boys to death; after their interment the neighborhood for miles around donated as liberally as they could to a fund to replace the building lost by fire. At this time the H[—]s had only five dollars, with no hopes of getting more money soon; they discussed the situation of their neighbors who had lost their home by fire and freely turned the $5.00 over to the soliciting committee to help them rebuild their home, and immediately afterward Mr. H[—] borrowed some money from his brother-in-law in Kansas. In the spring and summer following, Mrs. H[—] worked out in harvest time, cooking for harvest hands to help make money to repay what they had borrowed. (29:280–83)

Cherokee, b. 1-23-1887

I lived on the eighty acres allotment assigned me by the Government.[7] My father helped to make the rolls for the Dawes Commission, but died before they were completed. He had already been enrolled and his allotment assigned to him, but a ruling was made that if an Indian died before the allotment was completed, his name was dropped from the rolls and his land allotted to some other eligible Indian.

. . .

You may not have known that the first prohibitory law in America, now so common in state statuettes, was written in the law of the Cherokee as early as 1823 by an act suppressing the sale and introduction of ardent spirits in the Cherokee Nation. From that date until the final dissolution of tribal government the traffic in spirituous liquors was effectively suppressed by their own legislature.[8] (100:415, 433–34)

Anglo, b. 4-3-1870 Osage County, Missouri

We got word that my father was dangerously ill, in fact, not expected to live, so my husband and I loaded everything we could into our wagon again and with our two little ones who were just babies, we started back down in Texas to see Father. The roads were unworked and in many places in the creek bottoms the grass and reeds grew higher than the wagon and when we camped at night, we had our wagon fixed so that we could all sleep in it, for most all we had was bedding and our cooking outfit.

We crossed Red River at Illinois Bend; Courtney Flat was on the Territory side of the river and the little town of Byers was on the Texas side, but there was no bridge on the river and a very poor road through the sand roughs. We started to cross a little creek leading down to the river and after the wagon ran down to the bottom it, with the load so heavy that our pony teams could not pull it up the bank on the other side try as they might. My husband told me to drive the team and he would push at the back wheel and perhaps the horses could pull out.

The horses pulled their best but one of the ponies fell down under the wagon tongue and could not get up, so I called to my husband, who was pushing behind the wagon and he came around to the front. I saw at once that something was wrong with him. He had been suffering for some time with spells like palpitation of the heart and I always feared the worst for him. He climbed into the wagon and fell backward on the bed. There I was miles from a human being, only two babies in the wagon, and I thought my husband might be dying and one of the horses down and could not get up.

I forgot the horses and began to work with my husband and rub him; he always carried a bottle of camphor in his pocket for such emergencies and I found this bottle and applied the camphor. After awhile the attack wore away and he was able to get up.

We got the horses out and the team straightened out. Then we unloaded everything in the wagon and carried it on our backs up the hill. Then we hitched the team back to the wagon and drove on to the Red River.

Here a man made his living by piloting travelers across the river. He had a saddle horse that knew where the firm sand was to be found and the man would tie a rope to the horn of his saddle and the end of the wagon tongue and would pull the traveler across and he had a team there which he would hitch onto the load if necessary. We made the remainder of the trip without mishap. (31:271–72)

Anglo from Tennessee, b. 1890

I married Louis Armstrong. He was killed in an automobile accident in 1918 near Whitesboro, Texas. Our son is Ralph Armstrong of Vinita. He is thirty-two years old. My present husband is Dan B[—], a druggist here. (89:102)

Creek, b. 1864

During that time [at the close of the Civil War], exact date not known, my father made a trip to Fort Smith to attend to some property he owned. He was taken suddenly ill and died and was buried there. As travel was difficult and conditions so unsettled in the Territory at that time, my mother was unable to go and we never knew the exact location of his grave.

Being left alone, my mother returned to the Creek Nation to live among her own tribe and relatives. We settled at Old Town, near the present site of Eufaula. As we lived near Asbury Mission, a Methodist school, I attended school there and also Sunday school. I lived in that vicinity until I was sixteen years old, when I went north to school. (12:138–39)

Anglo, b. 1855

There were no doctors this side of Quanah (forty miles) and I have seen both mother and baby die for want of attention at the birth of a baby. We neighbors did for each other the best we could. (72:342)

Anglo from Texas, b. 1869

In later years I often had to stay alone with my children as our relatives settled on their own claims and moved to themselves. One time my husband had to be away from home and it was two and one half miles to the nearest neighbor. My two children were quite small. I became very ill, suffering with pains in my body. There was no one to send for aid and I thought I might die. I wondered what would become of my children if I should leave them alone. We kept medicine on hand and I took what I thought was best and doctored myself as best I could and the next morning I was much better. People had to depend upon themselves in the early days. (62:195–200)

Anglo from Texas, b. 1899

After we moved across the Red River, it was a year before we children saw a woman other than our mother; this was in 1877. We did not know what a newspaper looked like. When Father would go to Texas, he would sometimes get a letter from some of our relatives if there had been a death or marriage in the family. (100:406)

Anglo, b. 1862 Columbus, Ohio

We had dug a well sixty feet deep and were still digging and my little son Eddie was crawling and not yet able to walk. He was a mischievous little chap and when I would go to pick him up, he would crawl away just as fast as he could; I went to the door one day and he was crawling directly toward the open well, and was right at it. I didn't dare call to him, or to go after him because I knew he would keep on running from me, so I did the best thing inadvertently. I couldn't stand it any longer and screamed; that startled the baby and he turned and smiled at me. I didn't go toward him but knelt and coaxed him to come to me. They never did strike water in that well. (63:268–69)

Anglo, b. none given

There was a drought one year when we were living on the hill above Turtle Lake, I'm not sure just what year that was but I know it was before 1894. The crops practically burned up and the gardens, too. We ate so many navy beans that year that my mother never liked them anymore.

. . .

We moved west of Enterprise after about a year, over into what is now Pittsburg County and settled at a little place called Bower; a post office, three stores and a blacksmith shop. John McGill and a man named Ballard ran stores and a fellow named Barton ran the blacksmith shop. I remember he lived in a tent that had wooden sides and a chimney.

A man named Charley Howard shot Barton over a debt of five dollars; I saw the gun fire. Howard was sent to Leavenworth for ten years; our next blacksmith was named Levi Bruner.

. . .

There was a Choctaw family named Stanley who lived in a two-story house near the Canadian River. One year there was a flood and the water got so high that cows were deposited on top of the house and the Stanleys had a time getting them off after the water went down. (89:26, 28, 30)

Anglo, b. 9-9-1877 Fredrickberg [sic], Texas

Every year we had sandstorms and hot winds and once the wind blew sand for four days and nights until we had to take our food down into the dugout and stay right there and eat and sleep

until it quit. One of my uncles lived down on the sand and he had
to abandon his home until the storm blew itself out. When he did
go back home he had to take a team and shovel to drag away the
sand before he could go inside of the door. I have seen sand
mounds eddy up as tall as a house and as clean and white as sugar.
We used to climb to the top and roll down—it was great sport. Hot
winds were terrible. I have seen the corn in tassel when a hot wind
come and we would not even get a roasting ear. When a hot wind
starts it blows day and night and curls all vegetation like an oven
and nothing growing is ever spared. (89:63–64, 66, 74)

Anglo from Texas, b. 1897

We raised cotton, corn and some wheat. We had lots of hail
storms in that day and this hail usually got our wheat crop. We
didn't get much for a bale of cotton, but we didn't have to pay out
any money to get our crop gathered.

We had a cyclone in the spring of 1905, which destroyed and
damaged almost every house and barn in our vicinity. It took lots
of hard work to rebuild. We had to go some distance to get our
materials, such as lumber, wire and nails. (89:106)

Anglo from Texas, b. 1872

Oh, yes, while we were living in the tent, one night there
came up a wind storm and blew the tent down on us. We laid
there until morning, then all of us crawled out unhurt. . . .

The first spring we put in a sod crop, but got no rain and in
October we could turn up the sod and find seed just like we
planted them. The following winter we had lots of snow and our
cattle didn't know much about these canyons and would fall off
into the canyons in the snow. We have had some terrible times
trying to get them out.

A bunch of us went fishing one day and took our dinner. We
went to where Sand Stone Creek empties into the Washita River.

To our sad disappointment we caught no fish but we ate our lunch, visited a while and went home.

We went over in Greer County to see my brother and coming home the river was up so we couldn't cross and our horses swam across and left us. (89:135–36)

Anglo from Texas, b. 1881

Pneumonia was the disease that got Mother. In coming up Mother always had to sleep in the tent for she had already had pneumonia several times and there was great fear for her to get a cold. One night in stretching the tent there was much dispute about which was north for we always wanted the tent to have the door in the south for fear a norther would come up and everyone would get cold. It was cloudy weather and when the tent was set up the door was found to be opened to the north for a big norther came up during the night and we were really cold and Mother seemed never to get over this cold.

. . .

I became engaged to a dry goods clerk in the town of Loco and we had our day set to be married one Sunday and that Sunday my mother died so we had to put our wedding off for a week. When we did marry there were only a few very close friends came to the house and we had a real quiet home wedding. My husband took me to our home in Loco. He owned it. I had roses in my yard and a lot of other flowers and a nice orchard and garden spot. I raised a lot of chickens and canned lots of fruit and vegetables. I lived in Jackson County for eighteen years. I like it as well as the eastern part of the state but here I have to have a cellar to go to when a cloud comes for I am afraid of storms. (89:112, 115)

Anglo from North Carolina, b. 2-21-1868

Although the Indians never did us any harm, we were in constant fear of them. I believe, however, we dreaded prairie fires more than any other one thing. One could so easily become trapped in a prairie fire. The grass grew unusually tall, and of course was very dry in the winter. A strong wind would carry a fire on with great rapidity and fury. On one Christmas morning a prairie fire did break out. A small boy threw a match into the grass and was unable to quench the fire. Soon huge flames were leaping into the air and great volumes of smoke drifted with the breeze and the fire traveled in an ever widening area. Men from all over the country saw this and knew its significance. They quickly hooked up their teams, placed barrels of water and gunney sacks in the wagon and rushed to the scene. They fought all Christmas day before the fire was finally subdued.

Then there was an unusual burial that I remember. Old grandma Chisum died at a time when Bitter Creek was on a rampage. It continued to rise until the water almost surrounded the house. It remained that way for days. Finally the men made a raft out of an old wagon bed. They placed the corpse on this raft and swam across to higher ground, where burial was made.

We killed seventeen rattle snakes on our farm the first year we were here. I held my baby in my arms and killed one of those snakes with buffalo horns. (12:539–40)

Anglo, b. 1867

Late one afternoon an evil looking cloud appeared. We knew a storm was brewing, and made every effort possible to prepare for it. We tied the tarpaulin down tight across the wagon and chained the wagon wheels. A little boy came up and explained that his mother, living about a half mile away had seen us camping here, and knowing that there was a woman and a baby, felt apprehensive concerning our safety, and asked that we come up to her house and stay until the storm was past. I did not go, and we had a bad storm with lots of wind. I later became acquainted with this woman. She has always held a choice spot in my heart and our close friendship lasts today. She is the mother of Henry Kimbell, and resides in Altus. Her beautiful spirit in showing concern in some mere travelers was exemplary of the spirit that prevailed in those days.

My nephew, who was sixteen or seventeen years of age, joined us here, and we camped for a number of days. He had drifted down the creek one day fishing. I was at the camp, baking bread. Just as the bread was about baked an Indian rode up and got down from his horse. He looked around and seeing that I was alone, proceeded to raise the lid to my oven. Without hardly realizing what I was doing I threw back my head and screamed as loud as I could. The Indian dropped the lid, slowly mounted his horse and rode away. My nephew heard my cry. He thought the baby had fallen in the water, and came rushing as fast as he could. In reply to his question all I could do was to point and say, "Indian." All that could be seen of the retreating Indian was his red blanket flapping in the breeze. (31:160–61)

Cherokee Chickasaw from Arkansas, b. 4-3-1837

During the war [Civil War] we had to keep our food and bedding hidden as the soldiers would take everything. I would help my mother cook for the Southern Soldiers; we would get word the day before and we would cook bread and meat all day. The soldiers would pass in single file and take a piece of meat and bread but we would never have enough for all. One day we had cooked some turnips and had them hidden in the cellar when the Northern Soldiers came by and ate them all. We parched meal and wheat to make our coffee and also parched sweet potato hulls. (12:171)

Anglo from New York, b. 1850

On a trip to Okmulgee, my husband was killed accidentally. We made the trip in a covered wagon and he had placed his Winchester in the top of the wagon. We camped at the wagon yard and after he left the wagon I placed the gun on the seat. He came back and in getting into the wagon knocked the gun out, and it hit the singletree and went off shooting him. (37:215)

Sac & Fox, b. none given

Some time later, another Kickapoo came from Mexico bringing the black small pox with him. Indians died by the score. It was common for five of them to die in one day. The Hasquee village (located one mile north and one mile west of Rose Hill) suffered the most. Practically all the village was wiped out. The grave digger could not dig the graves fast enough, so they dug large holes and dumped the bodies in. The way the bodies fell in was the way in which they were covered. This mass burial took place on the banks of the Euche Creek near the village. One can walk along there now and see evidence of it. Every now and then you will find a human bone, and some of the mounds are still recognizable.

There was another small pox epidemic two or three years before the World War that wiped out a lot of the Sac and Foxes. Then the influenza epidemic during the war took some more until there are not many of us left. (3:566)

Anglo, b. 1868

I remember one funeral; an old Indian had lived on the place where we lived, and he was crippled and could not get around. We children would go every hour in the hot afternoon and draw a cool drink of water from the well for him, and when he died they took him to the grave and as he had a paint horse, (pinto) after the body was placed in the large grave this spotted horse was led up to the open grave with his head right near the feet of the old man. Then some Indian shot the horse, and it fell at the edge of the grave. A rope was placed on the horse's neck and they pushed and pulled that horse right in on top of the body. The whole bunch of Indians then filed around the grave and threw in some small articles which looked like beans. They had small pieces of white cloth similar to our handkerchiefs. These they dipped in the blood of the horse. These small pieces of cloth with just a drop of blood on them, they folded carefully and placed in their pockets or in their clothing somewhere. All the old man's clothing was placed in the grave also. He had some money put away and there was supposed to be a small piece of paper inside his shirt telling where it was hidden. But after he was dead, this paper could not be found. A German girl and I found it under the boards in the floor. There was $1,700.00 hidden there. I saw many other Indians buried and the clothing, trinkets, blankets and dishes would be placed in the grave, if they were not too large. Most always the favorite animal would be killed and placed in, or on the grave. Sometimes this would be a dog or horse.

My uncle had a magnet that located coins or metal. We took this one time and went to the grave of a small child where we knew that there was some metal in the grave and we dug in and found a can of old coins. I had never seen anything like them. We took them home, but Father made us take them back and bury them where we had found them. (80:272–74)

Miami from Indiana, b. 1877

I have grandchildren. This month we lost two within a week of each other. They buried Tiny's baby here at the old Indian burial ground. (4:80)

Anglo, b. 1874

We had only been in this country a short time when my little niece drank some poison medicine and died and her casket was made of boards, just rough lumber, and covered with lath. In April my oldest brother's wife died and about two years later, my youngest brother's little boy was drowned; their caskets were also made out of rough boards. These deaths left us very sad. But, of course, we had to carry on. (85:82)

Modoc from Oregon, b. 1872

My parents were brought with the Modocs from Oregon in 1875 when I was three years old. I do not remember either of them as both were of those Modocs who died soon after their arrival and they are buried in two of the rows of unmarked graves in the Modoc cemetery. I do not even know which ones are their graves.

The Modoc cemetery which comprises four acres lies just north of the church and is substantial fenced with a good post and wire fence and is entered from the highway on the west through a large frame gate of iron and woven wire. The ground is free today from any foreign growth and excepting where the graves are has been mowed this fall. The graves are in three groups which are on three knolls. Flowers and rosebushes and other shrubs have been placed at some of the later graves and are marked by monuments, but the greater number of the graves were made there in the first few years after the Modocs came when so many of the tribe sickened and died and are buried in a row or rather two rows marked by native rocks, but no one today knows one grave from another. (92:321–22)

Choctaw, b. 1878, parents from Germany and Mississippi

My mother's mother died when she was small and a Mrs. Horn took she and her sister to raise. She was so mean to them that her sister ran away and they never heard from her. Mrs. Horn would whip them with thorn bushes.

. . . She [interviewee's mother] was nearly one hundred years old when she died two years ago. At her request we placed her Bible, and a purse in which she had placed many little keepsakes; also a dress that she liked, in the casket with her. (29:25)

Anglo from Texas, b. 1857

There were a few graves on the first quarter section we proved up on, and Mr. H[—] [interviewee's husband] gave a few more acres, more than will ever be filled with graves, for people have nearly quit burying at Navajo because the grave yard is not kept up. I would say there are about three hundred graves there. (80:361)

Anglo, b. 1861

I have attended the Indian cries which were held a year after death. They served their pashofa in bowls with horn spoons from a long board table. Then, after the feast and the preaching were over we would go down to the grave and the women would do the crying in a singing, crying way. (12:412)

Anglo from Illinois, b. 1859

I never knew or heard of a cowboy that was buried on the prairies or on a ranch in this country. They were usually taken to Kansas, and interred in some old established cemetery if their kinsmen did not take the body to some other state for burial. At the burials of cowboys in nearby Kansas, a preacher was invariably obtained to officiate at the grave and all due respect was given them in every way. (107:443–49)

Cherokee from Georgia, b. 1840

In the early days on account of the varmints and wild animals such as coyotes and wolves being so bad, we used to bury our dead under the floor of the cabins. We placed all the little belongings of the dead with their bodies so we could not see these things about the cabin. We always buried our dead in the ground. I've heard about how other tribes did and even the wild Indians, but our dead were always buried as I have told you until the animals were killed off so we could bury as we do now. (66:16)

Choctaw Chickasaw from Indian Territory, b. about 1883

Grandmother told me of an exciting adventure she had with the Comanche Indians near the Arbuckle Mountains when she was a girl. She and a neighbor girl decided to ride to another neighbor's house, about five miles away, one day to do some sewing. There were very few sewing machines in those days and when a woman was fortunate enough to own one, the neighbors for miles around would use it.

It was a beautiful clear fall day, and as the two girls rode along they saw a herd of horses being driven by one man, whom they thought was the slave of the people to whose house they were going. The girl suggested that they race with this man as he drove the horses. No sooner was this suggestion made, than they were off at full speed. To their horror they soon discovered they were not racing with a slave, but with a Comanche Indian. They turned their horses around in an effort to retreat. The Indian gave a yell and a host of Indians appeared. The girls looked back and to their amazement they were being chased by this band of Comanches.

Grandmother wanted to jump from her horse and hide in the underbrush near the trail, but the other girl wanted to go on and try to outrun them to the house. Finally Grandmother felt that the best thing to do was to get off of the horse. This she did. The horse continued to run, and Grandmother crouched in the underbrush near the trail. The Indians rushed madly past her. The material which she was carrying fell to the ground as she jumped, and the other girl dropped hers at about the same place. As the Indians raced by, they stooped from their saddles and picked up the cloth. Grandmother was so frightened that she hardly dared to breathe. The Comanches continued their chase after her girl friend, and as she entered her home, they shot and killed her. Grandmother was indeed glad that she had left her horse. They took both the horses as they left. (21:348–51)

Cherokee from Indian Territory, b. 1851

My uncle in Texas was one of the meanest men I ever encountered. He had a lot of slaves and was just as mean to them as he could be. He would whip them at the least excuse, and they were as afraid of him as death. I remember one of his slaves had done some little thing to vex him, and he was whipping him with a long black snake whip. The poor negro was screaming with all his might when an Indian rode up, unnoticed by either my uncle or the negro. He gave a loud war whoop, lunged his horse at my uncle, hit him across the eyes with his quirt momentarily blinding him, snatched the poor bleeding negro up behind him and rode off. This made my uncle so mad at the whole Indian race that he said they were no better than the negro. (67:463)

Anglo, b. 9-8-1839 Illinois

We had lots of prairie fires in the early days. My sons have fought fires for three days and nights without sleep and with very little good. Sometimes the fires destroyed the homes and stock of the settlers. (113:141)

Cherokee Woman, b. 1887 Vinita

In the early days the country was really rough and tough. You hardly dared to keep a light burning in your house, or some tough would ride by and shoot your light out. I remember my dad used to tell us to pull the blinds down as soon as dark would fall or someone would come and look in at us. They used to come to our lot and kill a big fat hog, cut a ham out, and leave the rest. They killed our cattle or drove them off, as the notion struck them. One day I was hunting some cattle early in the fall, and I rode past some men butchering a beef, who never even had a milch [sic] cow, but I was a true pioneer and looked straight ahead, and never even saw them. In those days it didn't pay to see too much, or to talk too much, so what was a beef, when the country was full of them. (100:426)

Choctaw, b. none given Roebuck Lake, Choctaw Nation, Indian Territory

She [Ezekiel's mother] told him she would make him a medicine charm bag, a custom of Choctaw Indians years ago.

Ezekiel's mother then set about to make the medicine bag as follows: The Medicine bag is a mystery bag and is of great importance and meaning in the Indian's life, being constructed from skins of birds, animals, and reptiles, ornamented and preserved in many ways. After these bags were finished and decorated, they were religiously sealed.

The Indian carries this bag through life for good luck, strength in battle and assurance in death that his Guardian Spirit would watch over him. The Medicine bag was always buried with him, thus aiding him in crossing the great beyond to the happy hunting ground.

She told him to go and visit Elsie Beans, who had a goose farm and was called Queen of the Yazoo River and ask her for some white geese down to go in his Charm bag, and that would complete his dream. He did this and found her a very charming person. He related his dream and she gave him the down he needed. From this meeting a friendship developed, which ended in love and marriage. . . .

She also made a salve to cure external cancer from this formula: 1 pint of honey; 1 pint of butter; 1 pint of juice from green vines and leaves of the pole beans. These three ingredients were steamed slowly together until the mixture formed a soft salve. Persons using this cure for cancer must refrain from the use of alcoholic beverages, fat meats, or any oils, drinking few liquids only water, buttermilk, or liquid from Tom Fullah (boiled corn). (33:52–53, 62)

[Note: I know of one person who was cured by this remedy of external cancer when her nose was half eaten off. I witnessed this cure. —Field Worker.]

Anglo from Texas, b. none given

When we first came here I was very afraid of Indians. My husband took our cotton to Davis the first fall we were here, and had to spend the night there. I would sit and cry with fright nearly all night when he was away.

One day when he was in Mill Creek having his cotton ginned, a white man came rushing and said, "Please hide me, the Indians are after me, and will kill me if they catch me." The gin man hid him behind the cotton. When the Indians came riding up in search of him, they were told that he had gone in another direction and they rode off looking for him. I didn't know why the Indians were trying to kill him, very likely because he had stolen something or harmed them, but I got the idea that they chased white people for the fun of it, which I found out later was not true at all. I found them to be fine, loyal neighbors.

About the worst scare I had regarding Indians was one day while my husband was in the woods doing some clearing. An Indian and a white man came to the door and asked for Mr. S[—] [her husband] I told them where he was. They talked in Indian and made many signs which I couldn't understand. After they were gone I told the children to stay in the house, keep the door shut, and not open it for anybody. Then I ran as fast as I could to where he was and told him he had better hide. I just knew that Indian was going to kill him. He laughed at me, but I wouldn't go back to the house without him. The Indian didn't come to the field. I later told a neighbor of my fright and he laughed and said, "Why that was the permit collector and he decided he wouldn't go to the field after Mr. S[—]'s permit."

Another frightful night for us was when Mr. S[—] went to gin at Mill Creek and didn't get back. He was gone for two and a half days. The children and I cried most of the time. I was sure the Indians had gotten him. One day after he was gone two nights, I started to a neighbor's to tell them of my plight, and I saw him coming in the distance. I hastened to meet him and he told me that the gin broke down while they were ginning his cotton. Some of it was in the press, some in the stand and some in the wagon and he couldn't get away. So he had to stay two days until it was repaired. (80:101–102)

FIVE

Coping with Lawlessness

Violence was a fact of life in the early years of the Twin Territories. After all, sixteen-year-old Lena had married the older white Texan because the bride-price he offered convinced her Choctaw parents that he had the means to protect her.

Violence began with the horrors of Removal. The tribes forcibly relocated by the federal government into eastern Oklahoma were viewed "as invaders rather than bearers of anything worthwhile, save the guns and other manufactured goods the Plains Indians might acquire through raids or trade."[1] After their arrival, citizens of these tribes lived with the constant threat of trouble from the Plains Indians on the border between eastern and western Oklahoma.

During the years leading up to the Civil War, the removed tribes re-created patterns of orderly civic life. Then the United States' Civil War came to Indian Territory and visited terrible devastation on the people. Angie Debo notes that "With Arkansas on the east, Texas on the south, and vast unsettled areas of Texas and Kansas on the west and north, they [the citizens of Indian Territory] were entirely cut off from the United States."[2] Raiders came in from all sides of the area. Both Union and Confederate troops ranged up and down eastern Oklahoma, taking food stores, destroying livestock, burning buildings, and killing people. Families and tribal groups were divided by the war with dreadful results.

As part of the postwar peace agreements between the tribes of Indian Territory and the federal government, railroads were allowed into Oklahoma. With the railroads came non-Indian immigrants. A number of towns were bypassed, and new towns were established on the rail line. Most towns and especially towns on the rail lines were full of strangers, many of whom had little regard for the law and were looking for easy money. Violence grew more common, and jurisdiction became a problem.

Specific tribal Lighthorsemen had jurisdiction over specific tribal members, for example, Cherokees over Cherokees, Choctaws over Choctaws, and so on. Indian on white, white on white, and white on Indian violence fell under the authority of the federal courts, which operated first out of Fort Smith, Arkansas, and later out of Texas, Kansas, and Indian Territory (at Muskogee). These courts were located many miles from and, in all but one case, across state borders from the populations they served.[3] In a nutshell, Indian Territory was a good place for outlaws to lose themselves.

The lawlessness of the area was a major rallying point for whites both in the territory and on its borders, and their voices added to the clamor to open the land to white settlement. The Unassigned Lands (land left over after the 1866 Creek and Seminole cessions) were opened to non-Indians in 1889, and thus began a period during which lands were opened to white settlement. Oklahoma Territory was organized in 1890.

Most American Indians viewed this opening of Indian lands to non-Indians as a betrayal of promises made by the federal government in a series of treaties. Adding to the sense of betrayal, because of white political pressures both in Indian Territory and in Washington, D.C., in 1889 Congress passed a law requiring the parceling out of Indian lands (allotment) to Indians. Members of the Five Tribes were excluded from this action until 1893. The tribes resisted such action in varying degrees but finally submitted to enrollment and the resulting allotment.

Like the time periods leading up to it, the time from 1889 on was fraught with danger. Outlaws rode through Oklahoma on their way to rob the trains and banks of Arkansas, Texas, and Kansas (and points east and north). Killings were common, as were stabbings, accidental deaths by guns, and torture carried out in quest of hidden wealth. Even church gatherings were not safe from intruders. In 1893 more than a hundred thousand land-hungry people rushed feverishly into the Cherokee Outlet in the oppressive September heat of Oklahoma, and claim jumpers boasted of scaring off earlier stakeholders.[4]

The people who made the run and remained in the land established political patterns that have persisted into modern times. Lands bordering Kansas and Missouri were claimed by people with ties to the North and the Union. Land bordering the Red River attracted former Confederate sympathizers and became Southern in its outlook. In fact, to older native Oklahomans, southeastern Oklahoma is known as "Little Dixie," the north as "Jayhawker Country." Tensions were high because of differences born in ancient feuds, a sense of betrayal, and memories of war. Death was always just a breath away.

While chaos permeates the record of Indian Territory and early Oklahoma, along with the turbulence was compassion. Women helped each other in childbirth. Some people went to the aid of strangers, especially to the aid of women and children. Assisting others often put the helper at risk.

Violence erupted in the lives of women in Indian Territory and early Oklahoma and contributed to the stresses under which women lived. The stress came to them because of diseases, outlawry, bootlegging, domestic violence, feuds rooted in ancient arguments, and grudges held over from the Civil War. Tensions built just under the surface and erupted without warning, often with dire consequences.

Choctaw, b. 1-30-1829

[Interviewer Amelia F. Harris was given this interview on August 8, 1937. It was dictated in 1913 when the interviewee was eighty-four years old. Harris included this with her interviews for the Indian Pioneer Papers project.]

Cholera was raging in New Orleans, and we were anxious to take the first boat out. It was an old boat and not a very safe one, by the name of Alvardo. We had not gone up the Mississippi very far, when we found we were not in a first-class boat. Never the less, we would have taken anything to get away from the cholera. We found that nearly all the officers and hands were thieves. We had a single brother along, and they broke into his trunk and stole a number of articles. After this, he brought his money and gave it to one of my sisters saying, "I sleep so soundly I am afraid I'll be robbed." We kept this very quiet, and kept a watch out. One night we saw one of the captain's boys with a little fancy hat that my mother had sent to my brother's little boy who lived in the west. Then my husband and my sister's husband went to the captain and said, "Here is the one who had broken into our brother's trunk." So, the captain made the boy produce all the little trinkets and things that belonged to my brother. We had very great fear, for we knew we were among a den of thieves. (28:3)

Choctaw freedwoman, b. 1859

I was born in the town of Eufaula, in Eufaula County in the year of 1859, and now live one mile north, one mile west, and a half mile north of Okmulgee, in Okmulgee County. I an one-fourth Choctaw and colored. Although a freedman, I did not receive any allotment of land. My father's name was William Stewart, age unknown, and my mother's name was Millie, last name and age unknown. Grand-mother and Grandfather's names unknown.

I have lived among the Creek Indians all my life and am able to speak the Creek language.

Among the outlaws, killers, and bad men of the Creek Indian Tribe during the Territorial Days, and the most dangerous and feared man was a full blood Creek Indian by the name of Wesley Barnett.

Wesley Barnet was forced to become a killer by his step-father. Wesley Barnett had been sent to school at Haskell Institute at Lawrence, Kansas, which the school is for the Indians only. While he was there attending school, his step-father who had been sepa-rated with his wife returned, and wanted to take her back as a wife again, but she knowing him to be a cruel man refused to go back to him as a wife again. This refusal made him so angry, he shot her with a pistol, killing her instantly. After he had killed her he went to his home.

Her son, Wesley Barnett, who was now at school, was told to come home to attend his mother's funeral and burying. When he came home to see his beloved mother dead, it is said he wepted [sic] and cried out aloud that he would never be satisfied till he had avenged his mother's death. He went armed with a rifle to the home of the man who had killed his mother. Knowing that he was marked for death, the man also armed with guns, stayed in the house.

To the custom of the Lighthorse, Wesley Barnett waited around the man's house day and night for a week until his step-father came out of the house. Then as he had said he would kill his man, Barnett shot his step-father again and again after he was already dead. Knowing the man was cruel, Barnett was never apprehended. Thus he lived the life of a man of sorrow for twelve years always thinking of his mother.

After wandering around for twelve years, he had married an Indian woman. One day an Indian Stomp dance was to be held at Eufaula. He decided to attend the dance; as he was about to leave on a horse, his wife also wanted to go to the dance. He told her to stay home and a heated argument ensued, but being the husband, he left his wife at home and went to the dance. As he had arrived at the dance ground and was talking to his friends, his brother and his [Barnett's] wife came up in a wagon; seeing this made him very angry.

After attending to the horses, his brother went to the well or spring nearby to drink. Barnett came up behind and shot him dead. He knew now that he could not beat the Indian and white law who were after him for murder. He came into Okmulgee and bought a coffin for his now dead brother and one coffin for himself. He took his coffin home expecting to be killed as he would never give up or be taken alive.

He wandered around and among the Indians for two years after the killing of his brother. One night he rode in Okmulgee; as he was riding by the Creek Council House, he saw the eagle that is perched on top of the building shining in the moonlight; he shot at it with a gun, hitting it once in the wing. He joined a gang of train robbers. While counting money one day, west of Preston, the law surprised them; one of the gang was captured, others and himself getting away on his trained horse.

His horse was trained to warn his master at the least noise of approaching danger. His horse warned him by stamping its front feet. Before the gang was aware of danger, he was speeding away on his horse. Fast as his horse was, he was pursued by three white laws. He turned around on his horse and shot and killed the three laws dead with a Winchester rifle. Then he went to Arkansas as trying to escape from the laws.

The laws in Arkansas were notified of his being there in Arkansas. He somehow escaped capture and returned to his home near or about three miles southwest of Eram. The laws although anxious to capture him could not learn of his hiding place. He was now staying with his wife at the place just mentioned above. His wife being afraid he would kill her, told another Indian of his return. The Indian waited for him at his home as he had gone out. After midnight he came back home; as he entered the house, the Indian was hiding behind a barrel; as he [Barnett] came a few feet away, the Indian shot him in the face with a shotgun. He whoop [sic] and ran to his horse; he mounted his horse [and] said, "You got me." [H]e fell to the ground dead. His horse could not save him.

[Interviewer's note]: Wesley Barnett's daughter, Suzanne, was the first Creek Indian to sign the rolls at the Indian Agency in Muskogee. She was later adopted by Alice Robertson who was Oklahoma's first Congresswoman and Muskogee Postmaster for a number of years. (92:257–61)

Anglo from Texas, b. 1899

Some of these outlaws would come from the Texas side of the river and stay with us for two or three weeks, and they would sometimes offer my father money to get us the things we needed, but he would always refuse. He told them to stay as long as they wished, that he did not ask them any questions, and for them to treat us as well as we tried to treat them. They would thank him and ask him to say that he had not seen anyone of their description if officers came looking for them.

One of our neighbor families had a man named Blake staying with them, who was one of those outlaws who just drifted in and stayed awhile. This man, who had been in the pen several times, was sick in bed of pneumonia and three officers came from across the river to take him. This woman had a rifle and when they stopped and told her what they wanted, she told them that he was in bed sick and they could not take him until he got well. They got off their horses and were coming in, but she warned them to come no farther. One of the officers came a step too far and when she raised her gun and fired, he dropped dead. The other two picked up the dead man and carried him away and did not come back for Blake. (100:404)

Anglo from Tennessee, b. 1-18-1870, parents from England

My first home in the Territory was a log cabin of one small room and the kitchen was the big open world with a small tree for a cover. One morning as I was preparing breakfast, in 1889, a man rode up and asked for my brother, who soon came out from the cabin. The man soon explained his mission. Old Mr. Keys had been found hanging from a limb of a tree and this man had come for brother to help bury him. Keys had been hung for harboring horse thieves in the early days. Ropes and guns were the law; people paid no attention to minor offenses. Horse thieves, who were very numerous, were hated above all. (89:36)

Anglo, b. 9-9-1877 Fredrickberg [sic], Texas

There was not much law in the country at this time except a man's gun. There was a lot of stealing of cattle and butchering of cattle for the hides. Everyone had his stock marked and branded but stolen cattle were hard to trace and if there was a suspect he was summoned before the Grand Jury that convened only once or twice a year and there was many ways of getting out of going. Neighbors were not very near each other but we got to know quite a few people. We had some neighbors that there was more or less speculation about but very little heed was paid to it. One day one of my younger uncles was coming home a new way and came upon this neighbor butchering beeves that had the wrong brand on them and could not belong to the man who was butchering. Uncle passed the time of day and rode on without comment.

A few weeks after that this neighbor got a summons to appear before a Grand Jury. Of course he jumped to the conclusion that my uncle had informed on him and sent my uncle word that he was going to kill him on sight. My uncle paid very little attention to the message of death. One day this irate neighbor came by our place asking for my uncle and making great threats. While he talked to my father Mother slipped out back, bridled a horse without waiting to saddle it and raced through the woods to warn my uncle who was home at Grandfather's. When Mother burst into the house with the news, the enemy was coming into the front yard. He called very loudly for my uncle to come out while he himself got behind a big tree. My uncle picked up his rifle and leisurely walked toward the door cocking his rifle as he went. Both men fired but uncle's bullet found the mark going through the lower part of his enemy's heart while the enemy's bullet went wild into the log jamb of the door. This, however, made a difference in my uncle's life.

[Page missing] arm and one leg broken. He was a cripple for the balance of his life although he lived to be eighty-nine years, six months and ten days old. He was hearty and well, ate a big supper the night he died and went to bed and the next morning he was just not there. . . . (89:63–64)

Anglo from Tennessee, b. 1890

We lived in a couple of tents and in the smoke house until the house was built and I remember one night a dance was going on about two blocks away from us and we heard a commotion and shots and some fellow running his horse and shooting and yelling. The dance was on the bare ground floor of Bill Downing's blacksmith shop and a fellow was killed there that night and the man running off was the killer but nobody dared to go after him. We didn't attend any of the dances. And killings were of almost weekly occurrence.

They were so common that I don't even remember the name
of that man who was killed that night, but I remember seeing the
streets laid out and trees cut and stumps being blasted out. Now
that was before the railroad reached Boswell. That was in the fall of
1900. The first doctor in Boswell was Dr. Lynch. He came from
Mayhew there. I remember when a little girl twelve years old died;
she was Katie Downing, daughter of Bill Downing, the blacksmith.
They just took her out and buried her in a nice spot and that was
the beginning of the cemetery. The city bought the plot after she
was buried there.

. . .

And once a rumor was out that the Snake Indians were going
to raid the town and run the white people out and burn the town.
And that very night fire broke out. Those days the signal or fire
alarm was the shooting of guns. Some one began shooting guns as
a fire alarm but nobody went to that fire. That house simply
burned to the ground because everybody was at home hiding
because they thought it was the Snake Indians. The Snake Indians never came on a raid though. (89:100–102)

Anglo from Mississippi, b. 1870

In August 1913 Cole Younger, after he had secured his parole
or pardon, was touring the states, making public speeches to
young people in the churches to the effect that crime does not pay.[1]
In his series of talks at Atoka he spoke of himself and the James
boys as having a cave northeast of Stringtown, about fifteen miles
where these outlaws had lived for six months while they were on
the scout. Cole Younger said that this cave was located in the side
of a mountain with a small stream of water running near its mouth
and flowing east into Potapo Creek and while the outlaws were
located at this cave, in the late evenings and early mornings and
after a rain, the bobcats and wolves would come out from their
dens, farther up in the side of the mountain and play in the prairie
glade in front of this cave and for pastime the James Boys and he
would sit and watch them play. Deer and turkey would also come
to this glade to play.

When out of meat these outlaws would shoot some of these animals. This cave was located at the foot of the mountain and around it were large cracks and smaller caves. Above the one they occupied there had been a large boulder of stone that had fallen down in front of the mouth of the entrance to this cave that obstructed the view from anyone passing by and this cave could be reached from only one direction, from the south. While there, Frank James would go to the nearest town, Atoka, to buy their bread stuff, coffee, sugar, tobacco, and ammunition. He would travel at night to the only store in Atoka, which Jim Davis owned. This store was just north of where Atoka is now.

Sometimes Frank James would stay over with Davis until the next night. He always traveled on horseback and in visiting with Davis, James would tell him the story about the animals playing near their cave. So in later years Jim Davis named this stream and cave Cat Creek and Cat Creek Cave.

Northeast of this cave is what is known as Kennedy Hollow, and near the pot-hole of water is another location known as the Starr dugout and spring where the Belle Starr gang would hide out at times when they wanted to rest, and on the east on McGee Creek, in what is known as Booger Boo Canyons, is a place where the Mathews and Brown gang had their hide-out.[2]

In later years a fishing and hunting party went in there and camped, and according to the story told by Arthur Goad, he found $700.00 hidden in the wall of one of their caves where they had removed a small stone and had hidden the money behind it, then replaced the stone so that it was not noticeable. After the outlaws abandoned this cave, Arthur Goad went into it for shelter from the rain and noticed some loose clay on the floor beneath this stone, so he dug it out and found the money, so he took the money and kept it in his possession for several years before he used it.

This part of Atoka County is rough and rocky and mountainous with mountain streams, high bluffs and caves covered with pine and oak timber. Some places were so rough that one had to travel on horseback or afoot, and for those reasons it gave outlaws and robbers good places to hide and rest without being molested. (82:19–22)

Chickasaw from Arkansas, b. 4-3-1837

My husband's half-sister, Mrs. Willis, was going to see her mother to take her some quilt pieces; her husband sent a man and boy with her and said he would come later. She disappeared and a week later her body was found lodged on a rock in Little River. It was very plain that her husband had had her killed, but nothing was done about it. (12:175–76)

Choctaw freedwoman, b. about 1857

My first husband was a half breed Choctaw Indian. Some called him "Nubb." His name was Louis G. Folsom. I was his common-law wife. Our three children, all dead now, were Daisy, Emma, and Robert. Daisy was stabbed to death by Harrison Wilson, a Choctaw-Negro. Emma's husband shot her and she died from the shot, a long time after that. (31:49)

Choctaw from Indian Territory, b. 1869

In years past the robbers used to come into Indian Territory and molest the people. [T]hey would take coals of fire and burn their faces and punish the people in other ways, trying to get the people to tell of buried treasure and gold. (4:394)

Choctaw freedwoman from Indian Territory, b. 1861

On one occasion my husband entered the Council room and overheard Green McCurtain make a remark about him. He [her husband] knocked him through a big mirror and would have shot McCurtain if friends had not taken his gun from him. J. J. McAlester bought Mr. H[—] [her husband] a new suit of clothes for doing that job.

Later McCurtain employed two men to kill my husband, but the Indians thought so much of him that they told him about McCurtain's plans.

Mr. H[—] was quick tempered and always ready to fight; he killed a man for talking about his sister. The officers were afraid to arrest him and had a friend of his make the arrest while he was eating his dinner. He claimed self-defence [sic] and was cleared. (92:261)

Cherokee, b. 1851 Westville, Indian Territory

Early the next morning the Pins rode into the yard, took Uncle Tom out in the yard and cut his heart out, and him alive.[3] It was a horrible thing for us to see, and our only support was gone. Father was very ill and we did not tell him what had happened. That same day the Pins stopped at the gate, called Abe Woodall to the door and shot and killed him without ever getting off their horses.

Some of the neighborhood women told my mother that the Pins were going to burn our house that night and she carried my poor dying father in her arms, while I carried his feather bed and pillows to a cave near our place. Some of the neighbors brought our groceries, and sure enough that night our house and all we had burned to the ground. (67:452)

Anglo from Tennessee, b. 1-18-1870, parents from England

The law-abiding citizens respected and paid tribute to each other in gratitude. The churches and schools were made possible by subscription. At Community gatherings the men folk always carried their guns, at Church as well as other places. However, upon entering a place of worship all guns were taken off and stacked in some designated place until services were over and nothing thought about it, as this was a custom of the early pioneers and, too, a necessary precaution against the more dangerous element.

After some two years in the Territory and I had become more accustomed to the new country another surprise came. Only a short distance from my home a dance was given and sometimes during the night a brawl was started which we could easily hear and then came the firing of guns. Pretty soon, then, everything got quiet and the dancing began again. The next morning the men came over for my brother to help bury a man named Charlie Allen, who had been killed during the fight of the night. After he was killed they piled him up to the corner of the chimney and proceeded with the dance. This manner of law and order continued to exist in the Territory for several years and had it not been for the more refined citizens coming in and taking a stronger hold, this, no doubt, would have become one of the worst countries known.

I now live at my home six miles southeast of Blanchard where I have lived since 1900 and here where I have spent the better part of my life, I expect to remain. (89:37–38)

Cherokee freedwoman, b. June 1852

Father's partner in the tanning business, John Johnson, was called to the door one night and shot and killed after he had been asked for whiskey.

There was in that region, as in all other parts of the country I suppose, some men who did not join the army but who robbed and stole whenever they found anything they wanted. After the soldiers returned and learned what they had been doing during their absence, they took the law into their own hands and punished these thieves. There was one family that had been stealing sheep and the men, when they returned from the war, took the men of that family and drowned them. (106:446)

Freedwoman from Mississippi, b. 1870

In 1859 John McFields killed Jim Colston over some Cherokee money and threw his body into the Illinois River. They tried him in the Illinois District, found him guilty, and hanged him in the courthouse yard. In those days each district did its own hanging, but later on a National jail was established at Tahlequah, and all the prisoners were taken there to be hanged. (106:447)

Cherokee from Arkansas, b. 1877

For the most part Indians were friendly and peaceable, and, except for Jim Beef, Mrs. H[—] [interviewee] did not fear them. Jim, who lived near Sand Springs, was of a surly disposition whom many people feared because of his habit of shooting at the houses of those whom he disliked. This bad habit caused people generally to fear him. Jim finally married and reformed, but his bad reputation was of too long standing. He met a violent death at unknown hands.

One morning after a heavy rain his body and that of his horse were found floating in the creek near Lake Station. Those who gathered at his home opened his clothing and found he had been shot before his body was thrown into the creek.

Another such surly Indian was named Big Bird. Oma H[—]'s allotment which was west of Sand Springs was a part of the land which previous to the allotting had been held by Big Bird. Big Bird had never been reconciled to giving up his land and continued to sulk because no Indian was permitted to retain more than his hundred and sixty acres, unless, of course, he paid for it.

The H[—]s had rented part of Oma's land to a young man named Art Lewis, but Big Bird resented seeing anyone else benefit from what had formerly been his land and on several occasions had threatened to kill young Lewis. One night Lewis's horses got over into Big Bird's pasture and when Art went to get the horses Big Bird said, "Me kill you." Lewis was unarmed, but he hurried home, got his gun and when Big Bird walked up to the gate was ready for him. Big Bird sighted his Winchester at Art and was just ready to pull the trigger, but Art was just a little quicker on the draw than Big Bird, shot first, and killed him.

Lewis, who had a load of wood just ready to haul to Tulsa, went on with it and surrendered to the officers, but they, knowing Big Bird's reputation, freed Lewis. (62:156–58)

Delaware, b. none given

My brother, Albert Whiteturkey, was married to Jennie Johnson for eight years and after their separation, she married a Cherokee Indian named Gilstrap who was an outlaw. After he was killed, she married Ernest Lewis, another outlaw, who was killed Statehood day in Bartlesville, and then she married Emmett Dalton a few years later; Emmett was the youngest of the notorious "Dalton gang."[4]

The Dalton boys used to camp near our place and have eaten with us many times. They were always very friendly and nice with our family.

One day Mr. D[—] and I went to Bartles store for supplies and a Delaware, Frank Leno, was loading his gun to kill Gilstrap, the outlaw, who was reported coming to the store. Mr. D[—] tried to keep down trouble and when he saw Leno was determined and his efforts to reason with him failed, he took our baby and ran out of the store out of firing range. I also ran for cover and hid behind a barrel. When Gilstrap came into the store, Leno shot him, killing him instantly. This happened about one year after the store was opened. (2:471)

Cherokee, b. 1-23-1887 Vinita, Indian Territory

I remember one time my father and Ex-chief Thomas M. Buffington who were living on neighboring farms, had to go to Southwest City, Missouri with a load of wheat, a distance of about forty miles.[5] They loaded a covered wagon with wheat and started out and on their return, they brought home or started home with a gallon jug of liquor each, which was strictly against the law, even for their own use. A few miles this side of Southwest City, in the Cherokee Nation, they spied two men following them on horseback and, thinking it might be United States Marshalls, one of them slipped to the back end of the wagon and poured all the liquor out on the bran sacks. Chief Buffington wore long hair in those days and, being six foot two inches in height, looked the part of a dangerous man. The men turned out to be officers all right, but when they saw the old chief and my father sitting up on the front seat with a shot gun between them, they were very nice and, instead of searching the wagon, they rode around the side of the wagon, stuck one hand under the cover and said, "Guess you haven't got anything," then rode off. Not to be outdone my father and Chief Buffington drove on home, took two wide planks and stuck them in the cracks of a log cabin and squeezed out enough whiskey for their Christmas, and the hogs that were fed the bran got a little dizzy, too. (100:434–35)

SIX

Creating a Life

In Indian Territory and early Oklahoma people created lives containing the elements of lives they had left behind. This ongoing re-creation required that they build communities, and so they gathered for politics, worship, celebrations, and education.

The Oklahoma educational experience in the nineteenth and early twentieth centuries was complex. Tribal groups in the area prior to Removal educated their children in traditional ways. Girls learned from adult women by working alongside them in gathering, farming, processing clothing materials, harvesting, and storing food. They learned about herbal remedies, cooking, and child care and played games practicing what would become their adult duties. Boys learned the ways of hunting, war, and diplomacy from their fathers and uncles and, like the girls, practiced and honed their skills through games.

Shortly after Removal and until after allotment, American Indians had available to them public education that was tribally funded, as well as mission education supported financially by churches and subsidized by the federal government.

Before members of the Five Tribes left their homelands, they had begun to integrate white education into their traditional practices. This occurred primarily because of Christian missionaries. The Presbyterian effort in this work exemplifies the influence such missionaries exerted.

In 1820 Reverend Alfred Wright began working to convert the Choctaws before migrating with them on the Trail of Tears. In Indian Territory in 1832 Reverend Wright founded the Presbyterian Church at Wheelock, and by the time of his death in 1853 he counted 570 members. The Presbytery of Indian was established in 1840 and the Presbytery of the Creek Nation in 1848. When the Civil War began in 1861, the Presbyterians had six boarding schools, with eight hundred students, and six day schools. In 1861, there were sixteen churches with 1,772 members. During the Civil War, the schools and churches were closed when the Presbyterian Church divided on the question of slavery. The split delayed the reopening of churches and schools, but eventually they did reopen and began to attract pupils again.[1] The white mainstream education offered was heavily vocational. The intent was clearly to "civilize" the Indians.

To serve freedmen who had been owned by slaveholding tribes, the Presbyterians first established a church in 1869 and then a Sabbath school in 1876 and a school in a schoolhouse in 1878 at Oak Hill in Choctaw Nation that offered a curriculum similar to that of the Indian mission schools.[2]

Similar mission church and school patterns were established throughout eastern Oklahoma. Mission schools for Indians, such as Spencer Academy in Choctaw Nation, outnumbered those for freedmen. Methodists, Baptists, Roman Catholics, Moravians, and other denominations were active in Indian Territory. Converts numbered in the thousands.

Tribal schools, also numerous, were sometimes day schools and more often boarding schools supported by tribal governments. In the northeast, the National Cherokee Female Seminary, founded in 1846 in Park Hill, was one of these institutions. To the south the Choctaws and Chickasaws also established such schools, as did other groups of the Five Tribes.

Beginning in 1879 the federal government supported boarding schools both on and off reservations. Some schools, such as the Carlisle School in Pennsylvania, were off reservation.[3] Others, such as Chilocco Indian School in Kay County, Oklahoma, established by the Indian Appropriation Act of 1882, were nearer to the Indian homelands.[4]

A number of graduates of these schools became educators, while others became community leaders. Clearly, the schooling accessible to American Indians was sound, presented conventional white mainstream education, and was intent on molding the Indians to fit a white pattern. Some schools were coeducational, some gender specific.

American Indian young people who attended boarding schools both in and out of Oklahoma participated in the broadening experiences of travel and of exposure to new foods and behaviors not their own—teachers were usually East Coast whites intent on instilling in pupils the social graces and culture of white America. Sometimes these experiences were dreadful, sometime beneficent.

White children, because they were not tribal members, were not eligible to enroll in the mission, tribal, or federally supported schools. Still, white families desired formal education for their children. Schools for nontribal children were organized through subscription and were first held in private homes or churches. So valued was education that if a family did not have the money needed to subscribe, often it would board the teacher without charge, or its members would provide labor in the building of the structure or in providing firewood and repairs. The lack of access to public education for white immigrants added to the clamor of voices demanding that the territory be open to white settlement.

Education in the Twin Territories came not only from formal schooling but also from informal traditional networks that passed important information from generation to generation. Such instruction was cultural, its purpose not only informative, but also meant to counter information provided in formal schools, which, even in Indian schools, taught the curriculum of mainstream white America. Much of the information passed on in the homes focused on skills needed to live on farms and ranches.

Early Oklahomans came together for political reasons, to engage in cultural activities, and to raise money for various purposes—to send a delegate to Washington or to build a schoolhouse. They assembled for wedding ceremonies and Fourth of July celebrations.

Gatherings were in some ways quite integrated. White women sometimes attended tribal dances. Indians danced by invitation at white functions. People congregated at Indian agencies to collect government payments. Missionaries and churches held revival meetings that were not always but sometimes integrated.

Violence often figured in gatherings as well. Men carried guns to churches and to dances. However, dances were essential on the frontier, and family groups traveled long distances and dressed up for the occasions. Games were played during parties. Clearly the Christmas parties were very important because fund-raising events were held for many weeks in order to pay for them.

A sense of fun permeated such parties along with the work required to host the events. Get-togethers likely provided not only moments of relief from hard work but also moments useful for courting. Mothers naturally would want to see their daughters married to decent men in the vicinity so that they would remain near as part of the community.

Religious gatherings also figured prominently in the lives of families on the frontier. Services were held in houses, in abandoned saloons, and outdoors under brush arbors during camp meetings that sometimes went on for weeks at a time. These too required organization and labor in providing food. While the men provided the meat either from wild game or cattle, most of the work of preparation, serving, and cleaning up was performed by the women. Religious gatherings would also have provided opportunities for courting.

Any number of cultural activities took place in Indian Territory and early Oklahoma. There were debates, spelling bees, and literary meetings. There were musical recitals and performances by famous entertainers. The social scene in Muskogee included lavish parties hosted by Mr. and Mrs. Robert L. Owen, who included as their guests not only the young lady teachers but also Chief Pleasant Porter (Chief of the Creek Nation) and a number of eligible young men. Much courting may be imagined going on in the big houses of Muskogee.

In creating their lives, women of Indian Territory and early Oklahoma were energetic. They liked parties and parades; could, if they had the wherewithal, dress to receive notable personages; worked hard for what they perceived as a good life; and saw education as necessary for this good life. All the women seemed to have desired to create lives that they imagined, lives of purpose. Sometimes this meant lives of freedom. For some it meant lives of grace and refinement, interpreted in varied cultural ways. For American Indian women, this seems to have meant lives during which they could survive peacefully both as tribal members and as members of a larger mainstream community that did not always welcome them and rarely understood their ways.

Anglo from New York, b. 1850

I came from New York State to Ottawa, Kansas, moved to Indian Territory. I camped at Boggs, Oklahoma, during the opening of the Cherokee Strip. It was just like a big picnic; there was plenty of barbecue given free to everyone.

The Indians had their big "Pow Wow." They danced the stomp-dance by the music of a drum, dressed in full Indian costume. They also had horse races, riding bareback on little Indian ponies. (37:214)

Anglo, b. none given

As I had prepared myself to teach piano, I, as most young girls are, was anxious to make use of my training. I applied to various schools and colleges for a position. Fortunately, however, a long-time friend of our family, Dr. J. A. Anderson of Arkansas also a Methodist Minister, came to see us. On being told that I was anxious to make use of my training, he said, "I think I can get a place for you in the Indian Territory if you would care to go there. I will write to my good friend, Reverend T. F. Brewer who is President of Harrell Institute at Muskogee."[1] He did, and I secured the position as head of the piano department in a Methodist School for Girls.

The school at that time [1892] was under the Women's Mission Board of the Methodist Church and engaged largely in missionary work among the Indians, admitting girls who were called beneficiaries as they did part-time work for their board, helping in the dining room or kitchen for an hour or so each day. Their other expenses were often taken care of by missionary societies of Methodist Churches in other locations. There were, however, many students from prominent and wealthy families in the Territory.

The school was a substantial three-story red brick building with a dining room and kitchen in the basement. Reverend T. F. Brewer was president of the school and his estimable wife, who was lovingly called Mother Brewer, supervised the boarding department. They lived in the building with their three children, Robert, Bess and baby Theodore, who afterward died. Miss Frances Goodson from Kentucky was voice teacher, Miss Elizabeth Kilpatrick of Corinth, Mississippi, was chapel teacher. She is now Mrs. Burgin, wife of a prominent Methodist Minister in Dallas, Texas. Miss Bessie Wier of Starkville, Mississippi, was one of the music teachers as was Miss Fannie Locke, young niece of Mr. Brewer, who was a graduate of the school. Miss Cena Holcomb of Fayetteville, Arkansas, came the next year and was one of the literary teachers. Mrs. Sarah Reid taught in the Primary department for many years. It was one of the duties of the teachers to accompany the girls on shopping trips and on their evening walks, one teacher being assigned to the task each week. We could walk over, almost, the entire town in one evening. The social life revolved around the two schools, Harrell and the Presbyterian School for Girls, that later grew into the Tulsa University; but it was said that Harrell was the center of social life in Muskogee. (31:13–16)

Caddo, b. 1889

I was told by my mother that her father, James M. Davis, a white man, sawed and put up ice in a dugout in the winter of 1885 and 1886. The ice, which was cut on the Washita River, was about five inches thick. He cut about two tons and packed it in sawdust, that was gotten at the Government sawmill at Anadarko, on the north side of the river.

The dugout had a pitch roof made of poles and covered with straw and dirt. The door was made tight and wasn't opened until July and the ice lasted for about two months.

Before any land was broken, the river was clear and made good ice.

In the '90's my father, Thad Smith, had one of the biggest ranches in the Caddo Country. He controlled forty thousand acres of land which he had leased from the Caddo Indians through the Department of the Interior. He hired lots of cowboys who slept and ate in the bunk house near our house. One of our best bronco riders [was] Turner Cochran, a half Chickasaw and half Cherokee Indian. Nearly every Sunday was spent riding broncos.

After the Caddo, Kiowa, and Comanche country was opened, white men made quail hunting trips in the Fall and Winter [sic], taking big traps and nets. The nets were stretched up so that the quail, then gentle, could be driven into the traps. They were caught by the thousands, cleaned and packed in barrels, and shipped East for sale. (105:406–407)

Anglo, b. 1874

About 1898, my father hauled lumber from Weatherford and built a small house. By this time we were getting better acquainted with this new country but still it was not settled much. Our nearest neighbor was seven miles away and our post office was Ural about fourteen miles south of us. Most every Saturday it was my part to go to the post office and get the mail; I was then about twenty-two years old. I had to go horseback, but I had learned to ride over these prairies in a hurry for I have ridden over the prairie where Elk City now stands many times before there was any Elk City. We could sit at our home just four miles north of Elk City and see the tents and houses going up when Elk City first started.

When we first came to the Territory, our nearest doctor was at Cheyenne about twenty-five miles. . . .

Our hard times were many but in time they have been almost forgotten. My father and mother were getting up in years when they came to the new country, but it seemed so hard to have any-thing in the states, they came to get a home and for free range.

They suffered and toiled and went through many hardships and are both dead now. . . . [T]hey are both buried in the Grandview Cemetery. We children are badly scattered.

I was young when we came to this country, but now I am going down the slope of life, the mother of five children and a widow. I have watched the nation grow into statehood and from an untilled and undeveloped state to the present industrial and agricultural state of progress. This part of the country was all known as Rogers Mills when we came to the Territory. (85:82–84)

Cherokee, b. none given

My sister and I attended school at the Female Seminary at Tahlequah for the years 1882 and 1883. We were boarding students.[2] At that time there were about 300 girls there. The cost of board and tuition was $25.00 per month. We paid one half of this and the Cherokee Nation paid one half. Miss Allen was my main teacher and Miss Wilson was the principal. After two years of schooling at Tahlequah, my mother decided that the West didn't provide the proper environment for the rearing of a family, especially for girls, as it was entirely too wild. So, we decided to return to the East to our old home. (12:426–27)

Anglo from Tennessee, b. 1890

In 1903 Mrs. Tom Yeager started a subscription school in her home and she had so many pupils that they had to take turn about sitting at the desks while others sat on the stair steps. I finished the Seventh grade and got married at fourteen. I became a mother when I was fifteen and a half years old and went back to school and finished the Tenth grade. (89:102)

Anglo from Indiana, b. 4-5-1872

We bought our supplies and got our mail at Mineo.

We didn't have a school in our community, but Mr. Campbell, who had either seven or eight children of school age hired a private teacher to come to his home and stay and teach his children. (12:462)

Anglo, b. 6-14-1886 Oskaloosa, Jefferson County, Kansas

The first term of school I attended was a mile north [of El Reno] and was taught by Thyrza Still. The first school held in our own neighborhood was in our parlor. My father did not like the idea of voting bonds for a new school, and he helped solicit funds and work from the neighbors and so the new schoolhouse, in district 95, was built by subscription, and named by Mother. She called it "Eureka." A Mr. J. H. Hammond donated the ground for the schoolhouse to be built on and also his labor. Those who could afford to do so gave money and those who could not give money helped to build it. Mother taught the school after it was built. (89:162–63)

Anglo from Texas, b. 1897

We went to school at Plainview, a little settlement near our place. The school building was a two room house, painted white and we had double seats and desks, but only had one teacher. A[lmost] everyone had to walk to school, but in bad weather my father [or one of] my older brothers took us in the wagon. We took our lunch [illegible text] butter and bread, about two slices of country ham or sausage a[nd at] times an apple and we enjoyed this very much. We didn't get candy or any kinds of sweets or fruits, other than apples. (89:A1–2)

Anglo from Texas, b. 9-9-1877

There was an old dugout in the bend of Boggy Creek called Boggy school where school kept sometimes but we did not pay a great deal of attention to school. Willow Vale was the next to have a school. (89:68)

Creek, b. 1864 Boggy Depot

In 1879, Reverend Dwight L. Moody of Northfield, Massachusetts, who had gained world wide fame, saw the need of a school where young people of small means could secure a sound education;

such as he had been deprived of in his youth. His contact with people in every walk of life, not only emphasized the need of such an institution but gave him the opportunity to lay the idea before those who could help him formulate his plan and carry out his hopes. In the fall of 1879, about a year after the first purchase of property in Northfield was made, a class of twenty-five girls arrived to live in Mr. Moody's own home until the first dormitory could be completed. The dormitory that housed the students was a large brick building, the dining room and kitchen being some distance away. Nearly 100 students were enrolled the following year, 1880. Today, with 11,250 alumnae, 543 students, 79 buildings on a 12,000 acre campus, Northfield Seminary continues to offer a sound Christian education at about half the usual cost, to girls, who, lacking this opportunity, would be seriously handicapped.

There were three underlying principles governing the school; first, that the Bible should be taught, a part of the regular curriculum, during every year the student was in attendance; second, that each girl should participate in the manual work; third, that the cost should be so low that practically any girl could afford to attend and that scholarships for girls, unable to pay, should be available. These principles have remained unchanged and the graduates from this school girdled the globe.

Encouraged and inspired by the phenomenal growth and marvelous success for girls, Mr. Moody opened a similar school for boys in 1881. This school, which was located across the Connecticut River and known as Mount Hermon, has enjoyed the same measure of success as Northfield Seminary.

In 1880, Mr. Moody sent his principal teacher, Miss Tucker, to the Indian Territory to secure students for the school, offering the same advantages to Indian girls as was offered to others. Miss Tucker came to Eufaula, Creek Nation, and conducted examinations for entrance credit. They were given in reading, writing, mathematics, and history. As I was fortunate enough to make the grade, I was among the sixteen Indian girls selected to go from the Indian Territory. Only a partial list who went at that time is available. They were: Jeanie Ironsides, Cherokee; Kate Timberlake, Cherokee, (now Mrs. James K. Wolf of Los Angeles, California).

Jennie and Rose Yargee, Creek; Mary Colbert, Creek; Lydia Keys, Cherokee, (now Mrs. Charles Taylor, Fremont, Nebraska); Hattie Ward, Choctaw; Lonie Stidham, Creek; Ida Stephens, Cherokee; Annie Rogers, Cherokee; Ida Beatty, Cherokee; Manie Rose, Cherokee; and myself, Kate S., Creek. Fannie Keys, sister Lydia Keys, came a year later.

As we had to have a starting point, the girls from the southern part of the Territory met at Muskogee. A special coach was furnished for our accommodation by Jay Gould, Head of the MK&T [or KATY] Railroad System at that time. The girls from the northern part of the Territory boarded the train at Vinita. As no meals were furnished on the train, each girl was supplied with a lunch basket, generously filled at home with home-cooking. That was the last home-cooking I enjoyed for four years.

We left Muskogee on Monday evening at nine o'clock and arrived at Northfield Thursday noon. As travel was not as rapid in those days as it is now, that was considered good time. Our coach was attached to an outgoing train whenever it was necessary to change routes. As I had never been among northern people before, many things were very queer to me. Especially, the way they talked and I am sure we were just as queer to them. The cooking was another thing that was quite different. I had never seen sugar put in cornbread before and we Indian Girls didn't like it. Rice was served with sugar and cream as a dessert, where we had always eaten it as a vegetable. The school maintained a fine dairy herd and there was an abundance of milk, cream and butter. We also had plenty of fresh vegetables during the season. I well remember the fine chestnut hunts we had on Saturdays. Mr. Moody would announce that morning that we were going and to get the lunch baskets filled. He and Mrs. Moody often went along and always the teachers.

Mr. Moody was absent a great deal of the time during 1880 and 1881, for it was during those years that he conducted his evangelistic campaign in England that gave him world-wide fame. He returned in the fall of 1881 and that was when he opened the school for boys at Mount Hermon.

We were taught all of the home arts and spent one hour a day in the performance of our duties. We assisted in the housekeeping, cooking, serving meals, and laundry work, for which we were given credit in our school course.

As we were so far from home and railway travel quite expensive, I did not come home during vacations. One summer I visited one of the girls in Montreal, Canada, and another summer I went to Ontario, Canada. Those were very enjoyable times.

Many distinguished ministers visited our school from time to time. A large convocation was held there and ministers from all over the world were in attendance. We waited on the tables and I was amazed when they seated the negro delegates with the white delegates. Those in charge of the dining room service could not understand any reason why they should be discriminated against in a matter of that kind.

Once the Jubilee Singers were there and we enjoyed them immensely.

As we had students enrolled from all parts of the United States and Canada, they were an interesting group and we learned a great deal from each other. One day a girl asked me to go with her to the meat market and I asked, "Where is that, I never heard of such a place." And she said, "Where do you get your meat at home?" and I answered, "In the smokehouse, of course." I told her that we killed and cured our own hog meat in the winter and when we wanted fresh beef, we had one butchered and divided it among the neighbors. The neighbors, in turn, did likewise. We always had baked beans, brown bread and coffee for Sunday morning breakfast. The beans were baked in our own oven, but there was a public oven in the town where people took their beans, prepared and in the pot, on Saturday evening and went for them on Sunday morning.

While I was in school [1882], my mother married to Motey Tiger, a prominent Creek Indian, who afterward became Chief of the Creeks.[3] At the end of the four years, I returned to my home in the Indian Territory. I went by boat to New York City where I visited some of the girls who had attended school there. Lydia Keys, Kate Timberlake, and myself stayed the entire four years. On getting home, I at once set about to secure a school for I felt that I must get to work. I attended the Teachers Institute held each year at Okmulgee and was assigned a school west of Eufaula, which I taught for one year. I then entered college at Lexington, Missouri, where I graduated. On returning home, I secured a position in the Boarding School for Creek Girls, at Muskogee, which at that time was under the supervision of Miss Alice Robertson, afterward a Congresswoman from Oklahoma.[4] Miss Carlotta Archer and Miss Addie Willey, both Cherokees, taught there at the same time. Miss Aliee's mother, Miss A. K. W. Robertson, was with her then and they lived in the building known as Minerva Home. At the close of the first year, a call had come to Colonel D. M. Wisdom, Indian Agent at Muskogee, for a teacher in the Government School at Ponca Agency, and he offered me the position, which I accepted. The agency was located among, what was termed, the wild tribes, to which the Ponkas belonged. The Otoe Agency was near, as the Otoe Reservation joined that of the Ponkas. They, too belonged to the wild tribe. We had large brick buildings, comfortable and substantial. There were one hundred students enrolled. In the summer, the Indians lived in little houses built for them by the Government, but went down on Salt Fork River and camped during the winter.

The food for the school was secured at the Government Commissary and cooked in large vats. That was not very appetizing to the teachers. No attempt was made to teach the students table manners and the food was served with no regard to style. It seemed to us teachers a very poor way, if their intentions were to civilize the Indians. The teachers combined and employed a cook and we had our meals served separately, each paying their pro rata of the expenses.

We were employed the twelve months of the year at a salary of $50.00 per month and we paid our own expenses. We were on duty all summer unless a leave of absence was granted. It was against the rules for the children to be taken home often, and then, only with the consent of the superintendent. One day the mother of Dell Yellowbird, a little boy, came for him and on being refused permission to take him, drew a long knife from the folds of her blanket and threw it at the superintendent, barely missing him.

We visited often at the Otoe Agency as there were a number of white government employees there.

I taught at Ponka Agency from 1888 to 1891, when I resigned to be married to Mr. A. J. W. A[—], of St. Louis, Missouri. Mr. Ahrens was employed at that time by the Simmons-Gregory Wholesale Dry Goods House of St. Louis. We went immediately to that city and lived there for three years. We then came back to the Territory and located at Eufaula, where my husband engaged in the mercantile business, operating his own store until a big fire occurred and burned the building as well as the stock. In 1899, thirty-eight years ago, we moved to our present home, a farm adjoining the town of Wagoner.

We have two children, a daughter, Mrs. George Harrison of Sand Springs and a son, Henry, of Tulsa; and two grandchildren, the children of Mr. and Mrs. Harrison.

I have seen many changes in this country since my childhood, but with the majority of the Indians, I think, it lacks a great deal of being an improvement. (12:139–48)

(Footnote: Personal letter from Reverend Dwight L. Moody, Northfield, Massachusetts, 1880.)

Miss S[—]:

Your letter received and contents noted. The school will open about the middle of September. There will be a car to bring the girls from the Indian Territory here, without charge and free of expense. We shall expect to receive you as one of our scholars.

Yours truly, D. L. Moody

Choctaw, b. 1881

I was born two miles east of Nashoba, in Pushmataha County, in the year of 1881.

. . .

We did not belong to a special clan.

Nashoba had, at this time, one store, a post office, church, and school. Our tribe were mostly Methodists in the district where I lived. . . .

All the buildings and houses in our vicinity were lumber as there were several sawmills near by.

In school we made what we called the green book and I am
still in possession of it. We had board benches that we sat on; we
used slates and had a small black board. All the children who
attended this school were Choctaw Indian children; our teacher
was also Choctaw. (31:124)

Anglo, b. 10-16-1856 Indianapolis, Indiana

We raised our boys up there, fifteen miles from Doaksville,
north of the Towson and Cedar County line. We hired our own
teacher, and had school right in our home for a couple of years.
Then a few more white families came into the neighborhood, and
we got together and had a school house built. Even then Barney
paid the teacher, and my son Lee boarded her without charge.
She was Miss Della Kidd, now Mrs. Della Bedford, Court Clerk of
Pontotoc County, at Ada. (38:122)

Choctaw Negro freedwoman, b. about 1857

[Note from fieldworker]: The parents of Aunt Martha Jackson,
a black negress, and evidently almost a fullblood negro, were slaves
of one Sampson Folsom and his wife Kitty. Her father died when
she was almost a baby and she was too young to remember when
the slaves were freed, but when they were, she went to Spencer
Academy to do just any kind of work that they wanted her to do.
She assisted in the cooking, sewing, cleaning, and did just anything that a girl of thirteen could do. She went to Spencer Academy
just before school was resumed, after the Civil War, and according
to history that I have read, that was in 1870. So she must have
been born about 1857. That would make her nearly eighty years
old now. She was born on Horse Prairie, about fifteen miles southeast of the present town of Hugo.

[Freedwoman's words]:
That was the last Superintendent I knew [Mr. John Reed] and
I worked there six years. In addition to my work around the
school, I washed and ironed clothes for the teachers. I helped the
seamstress too. They made all of the boys' clothes, and they sure

dressed them nicely. They made their little jackets of gray jeans, and lined them, so they would be warm for winter. They fed them well too. They had men cooks, generally. One I know was Mr. Sam Pipkin, a white man. He was the best cook I ever saw.

The teachers were all men but they had women seamstresses. I remember two of the teachers were named Harrison and Penny-backer.

They had a commissary there and had just everything in it that they needed. Of course, they ran out of things, but would haul supplies from Paris, Texas. Sometimes they would have to get supplies at Doaksville, in the Indian Territory. There were always stores there, and they kept a pretty good stock of things.

There was an orchard at Spencer too, and they raised little patches of things to eat and we canned lots of stuff for winter eating. They kept milk cows too. There was a big spring down close to the creek, close to the Superintendent's house, and there was a milk house over the spring branch, and with a trough in the branch and they kept milk in that to keep it cool. The spring was all walled up so nothing could get in it. They tell me that that spring is so filled in that it is very small now and that the milk trough is covered over with sand and the creek is filled up so with sand that it overflows the spring. It never did then.

When school began in the fall, every boy was cleaned up and his hair cut, for fear of lice and disease. They were cleaned up good. The boys had to cut each other's hair. The larger boys were assigned to take care of the smaller ones, and see that they were properly dressed, changed and bathed frequently, and ready for meals, etc. The large boys cleaned and scrubbed their rooms, changed the linens, gathered up the laundry and took it to the wash house. Every boy was assigned certain tasks. Some waited on tables, some worked in gardens and patches, some cut wood, some milked, some cleaned yards, and then they changed around, took turn about.

We had a big bell that could be heard eight miles away, on a clear day. I heard it after I moved eight miles away. The bell was rung at four o'clock for us to get up.

We had alarm clocks too. We all got up and got ready for breakfast and when it was ready, then Mr. Coulton would always come to the kitchen door and tell us to be ready to come in the dining room for prayer meeting. We knew enough to put on clean aprons and be in there. Everybody on the place has to be there. The bell was rung again. It was rung at noon and at supper. It didn't ring at bedtime for everybody knew we had to be in bed at nine o'clock. Everybody has tasks to do until school took up at nine o'clock in the morning and after it turned out at four.

Mr. Coulton was right strict about the morning prayers and so was Mr. Reed. Mr. Reed would let the colored folks go into the church sometimes but we could never go to any parties or dances. I never went to parties or dances until after I left there.

The boys were not supposed to speak Choctaw but they did sometimes, as boys will, they sometimes fought a little and had to be punished but they were generally kept so busy they had not much time to get into trouble.

Occasionally one would take a notion to run off, but they always brought them back. I know of one little fellow who was brought back three times.

Sometimes when the boys would get through with tasks on Saturday, they were permitted to go fishing, or squirrel hunting down on the creek. The only game I ever saw them play was croquet. The school accommodated about forty boys and was always full.

There was a hospital room at the academy too where they took the pupils when they were sick. Mrs. Morrison was "Mother" to the boys and nursed them when they were sick and if they were sick enough to need attention at night, she took them to her room. She was still there when I left but she went away. (31:41–47)

Anglo, b. none given

We had school at Bower for three months in the summer time, and sometimes for three months more during the winter. We called it a National School, I think. White teachers were paid by the United States Government to teach the Indians. . . .

The Indian boys from around Bower went to school at Jones Academy near Hartshorne when they got big enough to be sent away from home, and there was an Indian academy at Tuskahoma, I think, for Choctaw girls. I know that Joe and Lige Beck, white men and brothers, married Indian women who were sisters and their boys were sent to Jones Academy. Lige had three sons; Milo, Grover and Green. Joe had six boys, though I don't remember their names. If you remember, there was a sheriff in Logan County just a few years ago who got a lot of unpleasant publicity for whipping a prisoner. This sheriff was named Beck. Well, that was Milo Beck, Lige's boy. (89:28, 30)

Caddo, b. 1-27-1884

I was born near what is now the little town of Verden, Oklahoma, located on the south side of the Washita River. At that time the land on the south side of the Washita River was claimed and controlled by the Caddo Indians, but later they were moved to the north side of the river.

At that time schools were few and far between. There were two Government schools near Anadarko for the Indian children. One on the south side of the Washita River for the Kiowa, Comanche, and Apache children, just west of the town of Anadarko [the Indian Agency] and one located on the north side of the Washita River for the Caddo, Wichita, and Delaware children.

These schools were in charge of white men and women. The superintendent was usually a married man, but a number of the teachers were single men and women. The Government schools were full of children. The accommodations were good, the food was supplied by the Government, and in abundance, such articles of food as meat, flour, beans, potatoes, rice, sugar, coffee, and sometimes dried fruits. The food was prepared by the older girls, under the supervision of a teacher.

The girls were taught to cook, sew, mend clothing, and do house work.

The boys were taught such work as is done on every farm, also carpenter work and blacksmithing.

The discipline as well as I can recall was extra good, considering the fact that the Indian children did not understand the English language.

The Government schools have been and are a grand success and they are more popular today than when first established.

The denominational schools were located near the town of Anadarko also, and it is an evident fact that their precept and example was and still is a wonderful power for good, and their influence is still bearing evidence among the Indians today. The Methodist, Baptist, and Presbyterian Churches, each supported a Mission School, for the benefit of the Indian children, and many white children took advantage of the opportunities offered by those good schools, without detriment to either.

Since statehood these Protestant schools have diminished and it seems to me a lamentable fact that we need them now more than ever.

The Catholic Church has a school near Anadarko, known as St. Patricks Mission and is still carrying on.

My first school was a subscription school in Anadarko. I was about five years of age. I boarded with Mr. and Mrs. Pat Pruner, good friends of my family. Mr. Pruner was a carpenter in the Government service. The school was held in the building known as the "Masonic Hall." My first book was a McGuffey Primer.

I took part in the Christmas program given by our school in the Methodist Church, and while the first verse of my recitation doesn't refer to the Christmas season, it does contain a far reaching lesson. I quote it below:

> If wisdoms ways you wisely seek,
> Five things observe with care,
> To whom you speak, Of whom you speak,
> And how and when and where.

I often think of this quotation and [am] glad I learned it early in life. (12:178–81)

Anglo, b. 1-6-1860 Ft. Smith, Arkansas

There were several Choctaw Indians that had quite a bit of education before they left the south. These were the ones that were selected to run the Choctaw Government in this country in those days; many of them were sent to Washington to intercede for the welfare of the Indian tribe. (27:151–52)

Anglo married Comanche, then Cherokee, b. none given

I attended school in town here [Lawton]. Now it seems that time passed very fast.

I married George Esadoo, a full blood Comanche Indian. He was a very small boy when Geronimo's band was captured and brought here and held prisoners at Fort Sill.

We have three children, two have finished Cameron College and one is in public school here now.

My husband attended school at Fort Sill Indian School and attended college at Carlisle, Pennsylvania.[5] Then he finished business college here. Football was his favorite game but once he was hurt, causing his health to start failing. He was very interested in our children receiving good educations.

We attended church at the Dutch Reform Church north of here where we were members. My husband is buried out at that little Mission Cemetery.

My second husband is stationed at Fort Sill. He is a full blood Cherokee. His home was near Porum. He received his education at Prairie Gap. When he was very small, he said their only church services were held once a month. His father was the minister. When his mother died, the people near them made her casket and his father preached her funeral.

We have visited my husband's relatives. They are of the Cherokee Tribe and they are cheerful and hard working people. This tribe seems to be more like the white people than any. The women wear little checked aprons all the time. Their homes are built of logs and have two rooms. These Indians have their own land but the soil is very poor and mountainous. I never saw any roads, just little trails over the mountains to the little trading stores of Porum. (15:420–21)

Miami from Indiana, b. 1877

Yes, I'm one of the last of the full-blood Miamis left. They had my name in the paper a while back. I was born in Indiana and moved to Oklahoma, near Miami, when I was just a very small girl. I didn't get much schooling, but I guess it was about as much as any of us Indian girls had at that time. For three years, I went to school in Indiana, and I sure did like it there. Then I came back home, and in about a year I went to Chillocco.[6] It wasn't nearly as big as it is now. There were just three buildings there then—the one for the girls, the one for the boys, and the one where we went to school.

They wouldn't let us talk Indian there, and I remember being punished several times for forgetting. I don't remember my Miami language at all, but I knew it when I was a girl. English is all I speak. (4:79)

Choctaw, b. none given

After grandpa died, grandmother made her home in the winter with Tom Hibbins at the home that she and grandfather settled. In summer she visited around, sometime she would stay with us till late in the fall. I know she was there a lot after I would start to school in the fall, and when I was studying history, she would tell us of the history of the Indian territory, and of their coming to this "wilderness" over the "Trail of Tears." She was old and had nothing much to do but sit in the corner and live her life over and tell us about it. She said that everybody who was able to, had to walk, but if babies gave out or the parents could not carry them, the drivers of the ox wagons would just take them and swing them against a tree and knock their brains out and leave them by the road side like a dog or a cat and not bury them. Her baby brother, Joel (who later became supreme court judge of the Choctaw Nation) was four years old and very fat. She was just eight years old, but she took her turn at carrying him because he could not walk much, and she said that she would get so tired, she'd think she was going to die, but she would hang on to him. She was so afraid they would kill him. She said she saw them kill babies who were too big to be carried and would give out walking. Nobody rode. Occasionally a woman was confined. She was permitted to ride for a few days. (24:38)

Delaware, b. 1862 near Lawrence, Kansas, Wyandotte County

I received my early education in a little Cherokee Indian school house located near Silver Lake, which schoolhouse was later used as a Baptist church, known as the Delaware Baptist Church, now Silver Lake Baptist Church; however, this church is now located a mile east of the original church. Mrs. Carrie Overlees was one of my teachers. I was later sent to a boarding school at Baxter Springs, Kansas and completed my meager education. We had very little education in those days. (2:471)

Caddo, b. 1889

I was born on the Caddo Reservation, ten miles northwest of Chickasha, in 1889.

At the age of six years, I started to a Catholic Mission school at Anadarko, Father Isadore being in charge of the school.[7]

The school was a two-story building; our sleeping quarters were upstairs and we girls, as there were eighteen or twenty to the room, were put in care of the Sisters, Tranquilla, Milliana, and Becarty. These Sisters were all young and were very kind to us.

One of our daily studies was Catholic Catechism.

Every Sunday when Father Isadore held services, several Indian men and women would come to hear.

In the fall of 1896 I started to Faits' Mission located about three miles east of Anadarko.[8]

My book studies were taught to me by Miss Mahan, and our Matron, Miss Langalier, taught us to sew and darn. Each child had a sewing bag, which contained a tape measure, needles, thread, pin cushion, thimble, and darning needles and thread.

. . .

During school term the Indian children's parents would camp on the creek, close to the school, and visit their children; sometimes they would stay two or three days, and it was a real treat to the children to go to their parents' camp and eat with them.

. . .

I attended the Washita school in Grady County taught by Miss Eloise Bell, one year; went to Almota Bond College of Minco, taught by Mrs. Sager, for two years; went to the Haskell Institute at Lawrence, Kansas three years, and finished my education in a business college at Chickasha, Oklahoma.[9] (105:405–408)

Choctaw, b. none given

My earliest recollections are of playing about the yards with other children my age.

My father and mother, Impson Jones and Jency James, were in the removal from Mississippi and many are the stories told us about the hardships of removal. We are Choctaws.

We lived near Fort Smith, but in Indian Territory. There were many Indians in our village and we children roamed the woods and learned about birds and animals. By woods, I mean the woods inside the Indian village. Far out in the open country there were wolves and other wild animals that would have torn us to pieces.

Many a time at night we would hear the scream of a panther. If we were not in bed, we would creep close to Father or Mother and be afraid to even speak. If we were in bed, we would crawl under the covers and not move for minutes.

. . .

We learned to ride quite young and to swim and paddle canoes.

The Indians were very devout in their religious beliefs, and taught us that the devil was ready to get us with his pitchfork for any mean thing we did. On several occasions when I had stretched the truth a little, I would peep behind the doors and under the beds to see if he was lurking around. In time I almost lost my belief in religion, but as I grew older, I understood.

After a time Father moved to Armstrong Academy. Father was caretaker of the capitol.

Our trading point then was Bonham, Texas and I obtained my education at that place. We went to school and church in a log house which had a puncheon floor and seats made of puncheons with holes bored in the ends and pegs driven through for legs. There were no blackboards and what a thrill it was to the lucky boy or girl who owned a slate and pencil.

While we lived at our old home, we believed in all the old superstitions handed down through generations. So of course we attended, when we were invited to homes where there were sick people and where there was supposed to be a witch doctor, or conjurer to cure the sick by the witch doctor to make them believe in their cures.

They practiced steaming the sick by cutting a hole in the floor and burying a post in the hole. The patient was placed on a frame and steamed.

After several steamings if the patient was getting well, the witch doctor would show something that had been taken from the patient by her magic, and which was supposed to cause the trouble.

I can still hear the beat of the tom-toms while this cure was going on. We children would sit in groups too frightened to play.

If one, by any chance, passed by the door of the sick room, he or she would be dipped in cold water to drive away the evil spirit.

We buried our dead near our homes so that they would not feel as if they were neglected. (25:253, 254–56)

Euchee, 83 or 88 years

[The interviewee] was west of Kellyville, Oklahoma [and] is 83 years. She was born near Polecat Creek and she belongs to the Long Tiger Band of Indians.

She is saying she does not remember her parents for she was very small when they died. She is telling me about superstitions about the Old Indians. There are lots of these old Indian superstitions.

1. The first one is about baby clothes. Don't let baby clothes hang outside during the night time for something may bewitch the baby some way.

2. Don't throw dish water out at night time for your grand-mother will get you.

3. Don't throw your hair outside on the ground for the birds will pick up your hairs and make a nest out of them, and a person will have a headache. And also, don't burn the hair off of any person for they say that when you are dying, God will punish a person who has burnt their hair. They have said God will make a person hunt all the hair they have burned before they can get forgiving from God.

4. When anyone out of the tribe dies, they say don't travel at night, for they say there are spirits here upon the earth and they will hurt you some way—that you never will get well of the sickness, whatever the spirits have done to a person.

So that is the teaching of the living person, yet it is still going on at the present time. (3:454–55)

Anglo from Texas, b. 9-9-1877

There was not much to go to but dances when we were growing up and mother was very particular where the dance was to be held if she let us go. Once there was to be a dance over beyond Willow Vale and some of the young men came to ask us to go. I said, "There is no use to ask Mother; she will not let us go that far." The young men said, "Leave it to me, I'll ask her." He would not let on that it was as far beyond Willow Vale as it was from our house to Willow Vale. Mother suspected something I think when we began to get ready to start so early. She asked me why we wanted to start so early. I evaded the answer for I would not lie to my mother. As we were going we noticed a big black cloud coming up and by the time we got to the place where the dance was to be, it was raining. A lot of the folks who planned to come never did get there at all.

We had to stay all night for it rained all night but Mother was not worried for she knew there was a wagon load of us and that we were safe for we had started so early.

Not any of us children or Father ever left the house without telling Mother where we were going for she always wanted to know just where we were and just about when to look for us home. (89:75–76)

Anglo from Texas, b. 1897

The only entertainments that we ever had were parties, and our parents always went with us to these parties. We had real good times in those days.

All the girls wore calico dresses, worn very long with lots of ruffles and trimmings. We wore fifteen cent cotton stockings and thought that we dressed up. We wore button shoes and didn't know what a pair of slippers were. We were better contented then than we are today. I have lived around this community ever since we moved from Texas. (89:3)

Anglo from Kansas, b. 6-14-1886

We organized a Sunday school right away and Mother was the Superintendent. A Reverend Patterson and his daughter, Miss Patterson, came there to hold services, and have stayed all night with us at times.

Father had a lot of stock and kept a good many hired men. The hired men did all the milking. There were many girls in our community and they had a lot of fun, running around together. The girls in my family had ponies and we liked to ride them. We also had a surrey and a buggy and were allowed to go whenever we wanted to, often going to the South Canadian River to fish or picnic. We did not catch many fish, but it was something to do and was always fun to play along the river. Other enjoyments were Literary meets or societies, held usually on Friday night at the schoolhouse, debating and spelling matches, etc. At Christmas time we always had a Christmas tree, with candy, nuts, and fruit, usually an orange or an apple, and the money to buy the treat was often obtained by giving a box social a week. (89:163)

Cherokee, b. 1877

Not long after this the W[—]s moved on to another lumber camp, this time along the Verdigris River near Claremore. It was here that they had their first Christmas celebration, the first time that the W[—] children heard of the old fellow called Santa Claus. Each child received a little china doll about five inches long and a few sticks of candy, and their joy at receiving them was unbounded. Minnie's very little sister Jennie thought Santa should come every night so for several nights after she hung up her stocking at bedtime, Mrs. W. each time putting a lump of brown sugar in it. (62:134)

Anglo, b. none given

As we had had no church or Sunday school, Mrs. Moore always conducted a Sunday school. In 1902 when my little sister, who had been born at this place, died at the age of three, and no minister was available, Mrs. Moore preached the funeral services. The little girl was buried on the top of a high hill near the house, a lone little grave. In my childish mind, I thought they had put her up there so she would be nearer to heaven. (1:192)

Anglo from Iowa, b. 4-5-1872

In 1891 Mineo was a very busy little town as the Rock Island Railroad was building through and was just one mile south of town that fall. Lots of supplies were shipped to Mineo and freighted to the near-by stores.

Mineo always had a celebration on the Fourth of July. The first one we attended there in 1892 was a basket dinner, with horse racing and dancing. Some Indians were there, too, and had their dances.

We didn't have any church in our neighborhood until we organized a Baptist meeting in 1898. We met once a month, winter and summer. In the summer we met on the river and preaching was held under a brush arbor.

In the winter they met at my house and had services.

W. B. Crocker, our pastor, drove from Purcell every month to hold services. (12:464–65)

Cherokee from Arkansas, b. 1877

Mrs. H[—]'s father always had a stand at the dances after he came to Tulsa where he sold ice cream and lemonade, both made at home, and candy. In later years he put up a kind of swing similar to a merry-go-round, having twenty-four seats, propelled by means of a man who pushed a long beam. Music was provided by a boy who was given free rides for playing the French harp. There was no floor under the seats, each swinging free and independent of the others. Frequently the motion made the riders sick, but it was a novelty and quite popular. Mrs. H[—] and her sisters were permitted to ride when any seats were not taken by paid fares, since her father, who enjoyed a good laugh, enjoyed seeing his own children get sick as well as seeing others in the same condition. (62:156)

Chickasaw from Arkansas, b. 4-3-1837

A Mr. A[—] near Caddo used to furnish melons to the Comanche Indians if they would come and dance for him; everyone would go. I went to one of these dances and was sitting in the wagon with my baby on my lap when one of the Indians jumped on the wagon and began to feel my shoes and my dress which had a design of large red flowers. I was frightened but I just sat there. Another Indian rode up and the first Indian jumped on the horse and left with him.

They had a young Indian girl all dressed in white with jewels on her arms and limbs and they were offering to trade her for nine cows and calves, but no one traded for her. (12:175)

Anglo, b. 1867

In about 1902 the Methodist Church was organized here, and services were conducted in a school house. I was a charter member of this organization. (31:162)

Anglo from Illinois, b. 1861

Sunday school was organized soon after we moved there. It was held in an abandoned saloon too. I was the first superintendent and held this office for several years.

When the people first filed on their claims, they were supposed to pay the government $2.50 an acre but so many of the people were poor and were unable to pay this that it was decided by the people of the neighborhood to raise money and send Mr. Kirkwood, who was a very enterprising citizen of the community, to Washington, D.C., to intercede with the government for the passage of a Free Homes Bill. The money was raised by giving a pie supper and a box supper a short time apart in the school house. Mr. Kirkwood went to Washington and did much in getting the Free Homes Bill passed.

The main amusement of the community was taffy pulls. The young people would gather in the various homes although the most popular place was the big dug-out of Mr. and Mrs. Lancaster who lived far across the road north of us. They had quite a large family of young folks and since Mr. Lancaster owned a sorghum mill, they always had plenty of sorghum for a taffy pull. They would cook the taffy in a large kettle out in the open. Then after the[y] tired of pulling the taffy they would gather in the dug-out to play games. There would be plenty of room for most of the furniture would be set outside. Such games as "Skip to My Lou," "Post Office," [and] "Scratch and Gravel," would be played. It usually took a day or two to get all the taffy scraped off of everything, but this was soon forgotten and in a few weeks they would be wanting another. (37:129–30)

Anglo from Indiana, b. 10-16-1856

We had a preacher who would come along [to Doaksville in Southeastern Oklahoma] about once a month and when he came we would have church and Sunday school. We had pretty good times. Pioneering is not so bad if one is young and healthy. (122:38)

Cherokee freedwoman, b. 6-1852 Tahlequah, Cherokee Nation, Indian Territory

William Penn Adair was a mighty smart lawyer and served his country as a Cherokee Senator and was sent to Washington to represent his people so many times, I can't begin to tell you how many.[10] It was on one of those trips to Washington that he died in the city of Washington and was shipped back to Tahlequah in a coffin. (106:444)

Cherokee, b. 1877

The older people of the community were accustomed in winter to gather at night at the home of some one family, build a huge fire in the fireplace and play games such as blindfold, hunt the button, etc. Always at such gatherings there was a taffy pull. In summer the men would gather on Sunday mornings . . . and pitch horseshoes or play marbles, usually staying the whole day, the hostess providing food for the group throughout the day. This meant a great deal of extra cooking for the housewife, and also that she had no day of rest the whole week through. Mrs. H[—] firmly believes that her mother shortened her life by the cooking and other hard work that guests meant on those days. (62:166)

Anglo, b. none given

In November, 1895, I organized the first Music Club in Muskogee. It was known as the Saturday Music Club, as we met on Saturday morning. Miss Fannie Locke, Miss Nina Jennings of Paris, Texas, Miss Scruggs, and Miss Bessie Wier, all teachers at Harrell, were among the charter members. I was elected first president and served as such at intervals, for twenty years, and am now [1937] an associate member. The club was instrumental in bringing the first great artist to Muskogee, Madam Nordica.[11] We were to pay her fifteen hundred dollars, which seemed an enormous sum for a small town. Each member of the club was required to buy at least one ticket at five dollars a ticket. Box seats sold for five dollars, then the prices ranged from four dollars to one dollar, those being in the "peanut gallery." The tickets went like wild fire and the sign "S. R. O." [standing room only] was hung out when the doors were opened. On checking up the next morning we found that we not only had paid Madam Nordica the fifteen hundred dollars but had seven hundred and fifty dollars to the good.

It was a splendidly dressed, fine appearing audience that packed the opera house on every occasion when a celebrity of any kind appeared.

The same week of Nordica's appearance, Madam Sarah Bernhardt, the most noted woman tragedian, also played to a packed house.[12] Other noted singers who have appeared before Muskogee audiences were: Madam Schuman-Heink; Tetrazzini; Calli Curei; [and] Sembrich.[13]

While the music club did not sponsor all of these fine attractions, they gave them their heartiest support. Several fine orchestras and bands came to Muskogee. Among them were the Royal Hungarian and Boston Symphony Orchestra and Sousa's Band. Madam Nordica made two appearances and Schuman-Heink, three, in Muskogee. It was a music loving crowd in Muskogee in past years, always wanting and securing the best. I am glad to have had a part in it and to have been able to make a contribution to the music circle of our little city. (31:18)

Anglo, b. 1851

All through my school life I remember how I loved to spell. I got a big thrill when I was past eighty years old. I entered a spelling contest at Coyle and was fortunate in winning it. The prize was a

beautiful quilt which I prize very highly. Mr. H[—] was the winner
in a similar contest at Kingfisher more than thirty years ago. He
was given a quilt as a prize, too. It seemed to run in the family to be
able to spell words correctly. My children were both excellent spellers
and my grandchildren were good at it too. (63:260)

Anglo from Texas, b. 1866

We also had our church. We had other entertainments here.
We had many ice cream socials and box suppers in the early days.
We also had lots of fruit suppers; the girls brought the cakes and
pies, and the boys brought fruits. (92:235)

Anglo from Texas, b. 1857

We did not know much about class distinction. Every one
was as good as any one else if you were decent at all. They had
singings everywhere and for years and years, every Sunday night
there was singing regularly at Navajo. Everyone went and sang,
too. There were no lines drawn at Sunday school, either. It was a
union school. Two and three times a year we would have a pro-
tracted meeting that would last three or four weeks. What a good
time everyone would have! Our young folks would go to the
mourners' bench and lots of them would get converted, and there
was always a good crop of backsliders for the Methodists. The
singing and shouting was always grand. . . .

We went every summer on the big fish fries where they seined
the creek for the fish and got all one could eat. . . .

When we heard the first railroad was coming through, we
got up a crowd and drove ten miles to see the men laying track
and the work train following right along with them. We had to
tie our team a long ways away and walk over to where they were
working. There were one hundred men walking along, some laying
ties, some laying rails, some nailing the rails down, and the train
coming along slow, slow right behind. I tell you, it was a sight.
(80:365–66)

Anglo from Illinois, b. 1864

There were not many social events in the country at that time; often, when a family was going to church or to some similar community affair, the entire family would go in the farm wagon, and if the young ladies had escorts, they would also ride in the wagon, the young couple sitting in chairs placed in the back part of the wagon. Sometimes "candy pullings," "pop corn," parties and such like gatherings were held at some farm home where the young people would congregate and have "the time of their lives." (29:277–84)

Cherokee, b. 1877

At the time Tulsa had its first Fourth of July celebration, Mr. W[—] [interviewee's husband] drove in the parade a float to which were hitched thirteen yoke of oxen, eleven yoke being his own animals. The float was constructed of two wagons, on the first of which was seated the queen of the celebration, Grace Mowbray, dressed in white with a silver crown, while the second wagon were all the other young girls of Tulsa, each dressed in white and wearing a colored band bearing the name of the state in which she was born. On this day, Mr. W[—] set the first flagpole ever erected in Tulsa, near Tenth and Cincinnati. (62:181)

Comanche, b. 1881

I was born on July 4, 1881. Years ago the Indians didn't have any calendars. They went by the seasons and different changes of the moon. The reason why my mother remembered the exact date of my birth was, years and years ago when Fort Sill was just a young fort, the soldiers always celebrated on July 4. Of course many Indians attended this celebration from miles away. Some few Indians took a little part in the performance. My father [Perdasophy] was away at one of the celebrations the day I was born. (82:140–41)

Cherokee freedwoman, b. 6-1852 Tahlequah, Cherokee Nation, Indian Territory

I didn't stay but six months with Colonel Adair before the Northern soldiers came [1862] and told all the slaves they had come to get them and take them to Kansas, where they would be set free and live just like white folks. They gathered up all the horses and cattle they could find, and the slaves helped drive them out to Kansas. They made a drive up and down Grand River and gathered up every "nigger" [sic] they could find and they had about one hundred when they left here, but had four or five hundred before we reached Kansas . . . .

When we reached Kansas most all the negro men folks joined the Northern Army, and the women were put to work in the fields just wherever we could find work. It was much different from what we expected. When we drove all those horses and cattle back from the Indian Territory, we thought they would be given to us to start out with, but we never saw them any more after we landed.

When they set me free, they made my master, William Penn Adair, a prisoner and took him to Fort Leavenworth, Kansas, where they gave him a trial of some kind, but he made them such a fine speech that they set him free and he came right back and took up his place in Stand Watie's army, where he fought all during the war. . . .[A] lot of other prisoners were taken to Kansas on the same trip that took us out. . . .

After the war was over, my folks came back to the Indian Territory in 1866 and settled on Fourteen Mile Creek, near Melvin, in the Cherokee Nation.

The Indians' slaves didn't like it in Kansas and most of them returned to the Indian Territory after the war. (106:444, 446, 447–48)

Anglo from Texas, b. 1888

There was preaching at the school house whenever a Minister happened to come through, or a man was sent by appointment.

Later, there were camp meetings where the people would build brush arbors at some convenient place and would come and bring their families. The people would put up tents or would build smaller brush arbors and make themselves camps where all who came for miles around were welcome, and these meetings would continue two, three, and four weeks. The ministers would take turns at preaching, and nobody thought of its costing anything for everybody brought vegetables, fruits, chickens, and meats or anything they had to eat, and nobody thought of imposing upon anybody else. (41:465–66)

Anglo from Texas, b. 6-12-1888, parents from Georgia

I did not get to go to town but about twice a year. We did our trading at Ardmore most of the time. At that time Ardmore was a very nice little city. There were lots of Indians around there. Lots of the white boys were married to the Indian girls.

I went to lots of Indian celebrations around Ardmore. My husband was a great hand to go to dances. The Indian dances were very interesting. They didn't dance as we did. I have also attended their stomp dances. We had just as much fun watching the Indians as they did in dancing.

My husband and I went around lots to parties and dances; the older people liked for us to go with the young people. We always went in wagons and buggies and took lots of wraps and quilts in the winter to keep warm. (21:238)

Anglo from Ohio, b. 1862

My experience with the Choctaw tribe was that they were against the white settlers marrying the Choctaw women, especially the fullblood [sic] women marrying the white man. This was permitted on some occasions.

Jack McCurtain, a brother of Green McCurtain, got a law approved that no white man could marry a fullblood [sic] Indian woman until he had placed fifty dollars with the Indian Department entitling him to what they called in those days intermarried citizenship. This of course would entitle the white man to the same privileges as the fullblood [sic] Choctaw Indian. . . . (63:268–69)

Anglo from Russia, b. 8-30-1884

Many years ago we couldn't get the Indians to come to church. We started out driving over the country telling them of services; sometimes we found the Indians in gambling games down on the creek; sometimes they would be holding a peyote meeting.

Speaking of peyote meetings, when I worked at the Parker home, the Indians used to bring their really sick Indians there to hold Medicine Meetings. The patient would be put into bed in a room away from anyone else; the other Indians would go outside and hold their meeting all night long for this sick person. If the sick person got all right, all was well, but if the person died, he or she was wrapped in several blankets and placed across a horse, then taken to the mountains for burial. In the days before missionaries were here, the Indians knew nothing but to bury their dead in this way. When the missionaries came, they taught them to bury their dead in cemeteries.

The Indians are very peculiar; if an Indian died in a house, they used to want to have the house burned, put the clothing and belongings in the graves, or burn them and would want their horses killed. Since the missionaries came, they taught them to remember their dead instead of trying to forget. (26:152–53)

Choctaw from Indian Territory, b. 1878

I remember, I think it was 1897, when Tulsa had its first big Fourth of July celebration; a great deal of preparation was made and one part of the parade was a team of oxen, consisting of thirteen yoke, which my father drove. They were hitched to a log wagon on which a platform had been built; this platform was about 10 x 16 feet. A bevy of girls and the musicians were on this float. My daughter, I think, has a picture taken of this team. . . .

I, being married to an Indian, attended the dances and various other celebrations.

One of the most interesting was the Shawnee War Dance. These were held at their stomping grounds near the falls of Hominy Creek. . . . At this point Hominy Creek and Bird Creek were about one mile apart. The Indians would go over on Bird Creek and put on their war paint and get ready for the battle. When ready, they would come across the prairie on ponies, yelling or otherwise acting their part. This celebration lasted three days and usually often ended in a sure enough fight. I know one time there were four killed; two officers and two civilians. The last day there was a good deal of drinking and, too, the Indians were tired and ill and it didn't take much to start a fight. We took our own food and camped through the celebration.

At the feasts and dances of the Creeks they used a table on which to spread their food while the Cherokees usually spread their feasts on cloths on the ground.

With the exception of the Shawnee War Dance, all other celebrations were orderly, about as much so as those of the white men. . . . (29:238)

Anglo, b. 1898

There were plenty of Indian dances of different kinds, but the one I remember best was the most common, called the Stomp Dance.[14] The Indians wore dresses or costumes of black or some dark color. All had short skirts or shawls wrapped around them. Their legs would be wrapped in buckskin or cloth, and above their knees they had strands of shells or metallic pieces, of tin, copper or silver, and these strands would hang down over the knees and jingle when they moved about. From strings on their shoulders they would have tin cups and from these cups they would drink the beverage from a large pot. They would collect a large amount of herbs, (weeds I called them), and these herbs they would put in a large pot over a slow fire and let them simmer. This liquid would make them drunk. While dancing they would stop and get a small amount of this every little while and in a few hours they would be staggering around and then it would make them sick and they would vomit.

The men would form a line and the women another, and they would dance for hours around in a circle. Sometimes the women would be on the inside and sometimes the men. They all drank of this beverage from the pot and all were sick. They had some corn bread made from meal, water and salt and sometimes a little sugar would be added. Sometimes this dance would last for two days. Some would beat the tom-toms and always there would be two near the pot waving an instrument something like a tambourine. These Stomp Dances were held for weddings and when Sun Dances or dances for rain were held, the Indians did not drink and get drunk as they did at the Stomp Dance. (80:271–72)

Anglo schoolteacher from Missouri, b. 12-23-1885

We used to have lots of fun in that neighborhood, as everybody in that community took such a deep interest in the school work and the literaries and box socials. When I went there, they had no library so I got up a box supper to take care of the situation. All the women and girls in the neighborhood came and brought their fancy boxes, and the men bid them up as high as they could. One supper brought in $50.00 and I bought good books for the school with the money. I taught three terms of school in Geary and was married to Alva L. H[—] in 1905. (85:99)

Anglo, b. 8-30-1884

After I started working for Mr. and Mrs. Becker, I would take them to the little trading post west of Cache, and go get them when the meetings were over. This trading post and agency was called "The Little Red Store." The Government was to make payments twice each month. The Government would notify the agency the paying would be on a certain date, then the agents notified the Indians. When the Indians received this word, they would leave their homes immediately and go to the agency, camping there for as long as three weeks almost. During these camp meetings, Mr. and Mrs. Becker (Missionaries) would go and camp with the Indians, holding revivals. Mrs. Becker was Field Matron, too. While Mr. and Mrs. Becker were away, I stayed in their home caring for their children, holding services and preaching the Indian funerals. When anyone needed help and I was alone, I'd do all I could and care for the sick, too. . . .

West of Cache there is a Nazarene Church called the India-homa Nazarenes Church for the Indians being built this spring. It is located in what is known as the Indian Reservation.

I have missed but very few Sundays being at the Mission since I have been here during twenty-eight years. My husband is a Mexican. I have five children, two boys and three girls. I live three miles southwest of Indiahoma. I drive over to the mission to help every Sunday and help Mrs. Becker work in her home during the week in busy times. I act as an interpreter, too. . . .

It was such a proposition to get the Indians near the church. Sometimes beeves were given to them if they came to church. I have seen some services held when only about six or eight were there.

Sometimes an Indian man would come in, wrap himself in a blanket and lie stretched out in a seat, talking whenever he wanted to speak, if it was in the middle of the sermon, interrupting the minister.

Many times in the early days, the Indians have brought their relatives here to Post Oak Mission for burial, when they wouldn't be dead. I cannot say how many times we have given the supposedly dead Indians some warm food and drink and kept their bodies warm by our fires; then they sometimes lived a little longer and sometimes completely recovered. (26:149–51)

Anglo, b. none given

Dr. A. E. Bonnell, a young dentist, had also located in Mus-kogee and was practicing his profession. He was quite a popular member of the social as well as the religious circles. However, he devoted most of his time to the pretty brown-eyed teacher at Harrell, Miss Bessie Wier, who became his wife.

Mr. and Mrs. Robert L. Owen had just completed their lovely new home on West Okmulgee Avenue. I think it was the largest home in Muskogee. They entertained lavishly and were especially nice to the Harrell teachers. Big afternoon receptions were the popular entertainments.

Chief Pleasant Porter [Creek] was a very popular member of the social circles; gracious, pleasing in manner, but always very dignified, he was a charming guest and companion.[15]

The first wedding march I played in Muskogee was when Miss Edna Carter, sister of Mrs. W. F. Crabtree married Mr. Walter Fears, a young lawyer. The wedding took place in the little Methodist Church that stood on the corner of Okmulgee Avenue and Cherokee Street. She wore a beautiful white satin dress and the longest train and veil that I have ever seen and I wondered how it was all going to get into that little church. (31:16)

Cherokee, b. 1887

That evening we really had a house warming. They came in buggies, wagons, and on foot for miles around, and stayed until morning, but who cared we had our house. We ate oysters and danced all night. The music was furnished by members of our own family. There were eight of us brothers and sisters and all played some instrument, and when we married off, additional musicians were added to the family orchestra. (100:421)

Choctaw Chickasaw freedwoman, b. 12-4-1880

I was born December 4, 1880, in the Box Spring Community three miles north of Doaksville in the Choctaw Nation. My father's name was "Pink" Thompson; he was born near Doaksville and my mother was named Lucy and she was born in the Chickasaw Nation.

My father and mother are both buried in the cemetery at the Box Spring Church, about three miles north of the old town of Doaksville. Box Spring community was made up of negroes. We had our school and church and Sunday School and a big cemetery. It was not far from the Nonnemontubbi neighborhood, was about three miles, and we could hear Captain Nonnemontubbi beating a big drum every evening and every morning. When he would first begin it seemed like we could not hear it so plainly but as he would keep on beating the sound seemed to just toll to us. We heard it all of our lives and paid no attention to it until we got to going away to school and when we would come home for vacations we would be listening for the sound of that drum beating up at Captain Nonnemontubbi's. He used to come to our house and sit for hours and we children would gather wild strawberries and give to him. He told the Choctaw name for strawberries. We would pick flowers for him too. After he was gone we would catch ourselves listening for the beat of that old drum. He must have been a soldier in the army. Everyone called him Captain.

I attended school at Box Spring until I was about twelve years old, then I was sent to Oak Hill Academy. It was a boarding school just for girls then. Before I went there and after I went there it was for boys and girls. Mr. McBride was Superintendent when I went there, but he died. The McBrides had five children, Howard, George, Greene, Rachael and Ruth. They all went off to boarding schools while I was there.

I was at Oak Hill Academy four years. Four years there entitled a student to a scholarship, or good grades entitled one to a scholarship in less time. It took me four years to get mine. I was so slow to learn. When I went to school there the main buildings were frame buildings. There were some old log houses there, which had been school buildings, but they were used for a laundry and storehouse when I was there. One of the main buildings was in the way of the railroad when it came through and had to be torn down.

At Oak Hill Academy, we played ball, checkers and charades and other games and sometimes Mrs. Haymaker and Mrs. McBride would take us picnicking and sometimes take us clear to the watermill down on Clear Creek. We would take our lunch and stay all day. It was only about two miles and we would enjoy the walk. The water mill was owned by Mrs. John Wilson, the mother of Johnny, Eddie and Raphael and Willie Wilson, all men who were prominent in the affairs of the Choctaw Nation. All of the teachers at the Academy were Missionaries, white people from the North. There was a small store and post office about a mile away called Clear Creek. We went there for small purchases, but all the big supplies were freighted from Goodland Station on the railroad.

We had chapel service every morning on week days. Then Sunday morning we had Sunday School and church and after noon Bible study until we had learned a certain number of Bible verses by heart. Then at four o'clock we had prayer meeting. They fed us pretty well when I was there. We had stewed beef for dinner lots of days, corn bread and sometimes beans, but not often. On Sundays we sometimes had chicken and dumplings and pies and cakes and on Thanksgiving and Christmas the school gave big dinners for the children over the country. That was the only time that boys were there, while I attended school there. We were not permitted to have beaux. Only when we were home during vacation.

For the exhibition at the closing of school each girl had a white lawn dress for the exercises, then they were given blue uniforms to wear home. These uniforms were usually of blue chambray, trimmed with white braid.

I attended Oak Hill Academy four terms and then when I was about sixteen I went to the Tuskaloosa Academy up about Talihina. Henry Nail was Superintendent. My father tied my grip full of clothes to his saddle horn and put me on another horse and took me to Goodland to the train and there I had my first train ride when I went to Talihina. I went there three years, but I never graduated. I was too slow to learn. But I like to go to school. I got out of chopping cotton and other field work. My daddy farmed and raised stock and rode the range for Mr. George Pritchard.

Oak Hill Academy was a school for negroes on Clear Creek about nine miles east of Doaksville, which operates now under the name of Elliott Hall. But they have negro superintendents and teachers now. Tuskaloosa Academy up close to Talihina was abolished because of lack of funds, and was used for a residence for years before it was finally destroyed by fire. The Henry Nail who was superintendent when I was there was part negro and part Choctaw. (63:314, 317–20)

SEVEN

Reflecting on the Experience

In the epilogue of *Women of Oklahoma, 1890–1920,* Linda Williams Reese discusses the *Pioneer Woman* monument in Ponca City sculpted by Bryant Blake in 1929. She describes the six proposed models for the statue's design sent on public tour and notes that "none of the representations suggested contributions by black or Native Women."[1]

This view excluding American and African American women prevailed for much of the twentieth century even though such women actively continued to contribute to the health of the state. Women, for example, excelled in early aviation and were among those chosen for the space program in the twentieth century. Reese notes that "for a brief time in Oklahoma history all-black communities provided an incubator for female advancement."[2] Wilma Mankiller served as Principal Chief of the Cherokee Nation and continues as a force not only in Oklahoma but also nationally and internationally.

Still, the image of the pioneer woman is white, and rarely do mainstream minds consider that pioneers were also African Americans and American Indians. That they were also pioneers does not diminish the contribution of white women in any way; rather the achievements of white women are complemented by those of their minority sisters. That is, theirs is a relationship of complementarity that enriches the heritage of Oklahoma. Also, while Oklahoma remains segregated in some ways, those separations have lost much of their force, and today one may see women of many races working together in various capacities in the fields of law, education, commerce, transportation, politics, agriculture, religion, construction, communication, art, and homemaking. Yes, women continue to create homes in Oklahoma just as their pioneer mothers did. They also continue to create the state.

We do not know if the restricted image of the *Pioneer Woman* monument is a matter of concern for women in Oklahoma. We suspect, however, that it is not at the top of their lists. Their lists are too long and complex for concern about a statue. Unlike the monument's restricting of the image of the pioneer woman to Anglo women, the interviews in the Indian Pioneer Papers make it perfectly clear that women of other races were here too. Fewer interviews with African Americans appear in the papers because those interviews were collected as part of a separate WPA project, reflecting the mind-set of a different and more segregated time.

The interviews we chose to include were selected not according to the race of the women who gave them but because of their value based on the insights and details that they could provide about women's pioneer experience in Indian Territory and early Oklahoma.

The interviews in the Indian Pioneer Papers clearly show the vital contribution made by African American and American Indian women as they pioneered alongside their white sisters.

Commonality permeates the interviews. For the women pioneers of all races, many foods were the same, as were the clothes. Means of food production were much the same. Generally, the women seemed content with what they considered their share, which included not only keeping their families fed, clothed, clean, and healthy but also included dividing any surplus with neighbors. Most differences existed because of socioeconomic class rather than race.

Women on this frontier learned to cooperate and live together, laying their fears of each other aside and sometimes becoming lifelong friends. Former slave women saw freedom as the reward for their labors and indicated the desire to control their lives. Indian women often focused on how they survived as tribal groups and spoke about customs adopted from their white neighbors. White women spoke of individual efforts to survive and prosper in a harsh but promising land.

Oklahoma women have inherited the traditions of women who acted as partners with their men in the domestic sphere long before they even had the right to vote. Women also committed early in the frontier's life to creating graciousness in a land that was fraught with hardship and that demanded unremitting labor. They did all the work required to provide food, clothing, health care, and cleanliness for their families. Then they worked a little more to make life agreeable.

We present these final reflections from the interviews without reference to age or race and invite the reader to consider only commonality as women look back at their experiences as pioneers.

We children had to work from the time we could remember and I can't see that it hurt us, but it would probably kill a child of today. (41:486)

As I look back over the years, I yearn for those days as they were years ago with their simple modes and the more intimate acquaintance of neighbors than we enjoy today. (4:181)

In 1908, when we first came here, Fort Reno was a more important cog in the scheme of things than it is now, as there were more soldiers and more activity then there has been since it has been turned into a re-mount station. Most of the Fourth of July celebrations were held in Peaches Park, later, after the War, named Legion Park. We came here in the horse and buggy days and have watched the town grow up until it is fairly well streamlined. (85:100)

Our family has grown up here and I have had many experiences in the new country. We now live in Lone Wolf and will celebrate our fiftieth wedding anniversary next November, 1937. (31:271, 275)

I tramped many a mile in these woods after my geese, and earned all I got out of them, but we pioneer women never thought of anything else but working and doing our share. (43:229)

Everyone felt the need of a Sunday school and as our house afforded the most room, the people of the community met there each Sunday for nearly a year. (63:259)

That was true contentment; our family were [sic] closer to each other and each one's troubles was the concern of the whole family. There was no rush hither and thither, one member going to a party fifty miles in one direction and another to church a few blocks away, another to a picture show, and some other member to a political meeting. When we went to a picnic or fishing, the whole family went. A new dress for one of the women or a shirt for one of the boys meant something to us all. There is no happiness without contentment, and we had it. Mother knit our stockings and gloves, and we women folks sewed on our fingers for the family. Some years later we got a sewing machine; that was a great event in our family. (100:404)

[T]hen the hard times began. El Reno was the nearest railroad town, a distance of about one hundred and fifty miles. We were here with no material to build houses, but we lived in tents and the men soon set about houses. Some of them were built of cottonwood logs that grew in canyons about twelve miles from where we were, and it was no easy task to cut those logs and drag them out of the canyons. Of course, this had to be done with horses, and then hauled to our claims over the prairie where the grass was waist high and there were no roads. (85:81)

We never had a doctor for confinement cases; the women of the neighborhood took care of each other. (100:404-12)

She said she was about 12 years old at the time of the Civil War. Her father was killed in that war at the time. This is all she would tell me. (3:615)

We had all the good things we could eat. There was the hickory nut hominy. Nothing could be better; and parched corn; and the beaten bread, and so many other good things. I have made them often since I have been a woman, but none of them have ever tasted so good as they did when I was a child.

I am old now and have lived a full life, but those good old days when I was a child are still dear to me, and the memory of them brighten many a day that otherwise would be dreary. (25:256)

The Kiowa Indians came over every day. I never feared them. Komalta and his tribe came often. One time more than one hundred came by on their way home from a picnic which they had attended at Mangum; this was about 1899.

We had good neighbors and enjoyed many things among ourselves. . . . (62:200)

This was truly a goodly land. Everything would grow. (89:113)

While we were Cherokee Indians, we had been used to a quiet and secure existence so the wild new country frightened my mother and she preferred to live in town. (12:426)

When we left our old home in Coalwater, Ohio, I was very sad and felt that if I traveled the world over I could never find a place I would like as well. But today, in our nice old home which we have lived in for twenty years, I can truly say I am enjoying living in El Reno and Canadian County as well. (12:107)

I never went any place, I stayed very close at home and knew very little of what the other people were doing or their ways of living.

I don't remember how we made our medicines but I do know we used lots of home remedies. (31:125)

Most all the neighbors we had were our kinfolks and the country was so wild that we women were afraid all the time when we camped out; I was afraid of animals and snakes as well as of the Indians, negroes, and lots of the whites. (32:272A)

It seemed that we were handicapped from the first. I had to sell our cows one by one to provide provisions. Our main food was cornbread and side meat. . . . (41:501)

There was hardly a house in the entire country, only a few Indian huts scattered far and wide. There was no land in cultivation so they [her parents] were truly pioneers, indeed, with high hopes and with hearts undaunted, with cherished dreams of the future, clearing the path ahead, they forged their way into the wilderness to build a home for themselves and their children. In 1882 my father, with only one old span of mules, hauled lumber from Spavinaw, a distance of about fifteen miles and built himself a new frame house, consisting of three rooms, one story high, and in 1896 added another story, with two additional rooms with a big fireplace at each end of the house. The old house is still standing and is one of the oldest land-marks in Craig County. My father died in 1900, and my mother March 1, 1930, but their works and memories live on. (100:116–17)

So, the pioneer dogs are entitled to be remembered as a very material part of the life of those whose history and customs we are now attempting to portray. . . . Yes, we must give the faithful and helpful dog a place in writing the history of this part of Oklahoma. (4:188–89)

The first few years were very hard indeed, principally because we had no start. We did not even have sufficient clothing. . . . If some of the neighbors had not helped us, I don't know what we would have done. They helped us in many ways, even to loaning us cows to milk.

I suppose our lives were similar in all respects to those of other pioneers. We lived in a dugout, as did many others. We made every effort to get ahead, and we succeeded. . . . Well, our pioneer days were frought [sic] with danger and hardships, but we won out and got our start in life. (12:138, 139, 141)

I had a very difficult time making a living for my family of girls. I rented the land each year to a tenant, and we tried to keep our part of the store going. Eggs were almost unsalable [sic]. Everybody had eggs and stores would hardly buy them, even at 4 cents a dozen. (113:399)

There was no one to send for aid and I thought I might die. I wondered what would become of my children if I should leave them alone. We kept medicine on hand and I took what I thought was best and doctored myself as best I could and the next morning I was much better. People had to depend upon themselves in the early days. (62:200)

I later became acquainted with this woman [a neighbor of interviewee]. She has always held a choice spot in my heart and our close friendship lasts today. She is the mother of Henry Kimbell, and resides in Altus. Her beautiful spirit in showing concern in some mere travelers was exemplary of the spirit that prevailed in those days. (31:160–61)

This manner of law and order continued to exist in the Territory for several years and had it not been for the more refined citizens coming in and taking a stronger hold, this, no doubt, would have become one of the worst countries known. (89:38)

Our hard times were many but in time they have been almost forgotten. My father and mother were getting up in years when they came to the new country, but it seemed so hard to have anything in the states, they came to get a home and for free range. They suffered and toiled and went through many hardships and are both dead now. . . . [T]hey are both buried in the Grandview Cemetery. We children are badly scattered.

I was young when we came to this country, but now I am going down the slope of life, the mother of five children and a widow. I have watched the nation grow into statehood and from an

untilled and undeveloped state to the present industrial and agricultural state of progress. This part of the country was all known
as Rogers Mills when we came to the Territory. (85:83–84)

> If wisdoms ways you wisely seek,
> Five things observe with care,
> To whom you speak, Of whom you speak,
> And how and when and where.

I often think of this quotation and [am] glad I learned it early
in life. (12:181)

On several occasions when I had stretched the truth a little, I
would peep behind the doors and under the beds to see if he [the
devil] was lurking around. In time I almost lost my belief in religion, but as I grew older, I understood. (25:254)

We were better contented then than we are today. I have lived
around this community ever since we moved from Texas. (89:3)

We had a preacher who would come along about once a
month and when he came we would have church and Sunday
school. We had pretty good times. Pioneering is not so bad if one
is young and healthy. (122:38)

After the war was over, my folks came back to the Indian Territory in 1866 and settled on Fourteen Mile Creek, near Melvin,
in the Cherokee Nation.

The Indians' slaves didn't like it in Kansas and most of them
returned to the Indian Territory after the war. (106:448)

We did not know much about class distinction. Every one was
as good as any one else if you were decent at all. (80:365)

Notes

PREFACE

1. Bataille and Sands, *American Indian Women,* 6; Hopkins, *Life Among the Piutes;* Linderman, *Pretty-Shield.*
2. Indian Pioneer Papers.
3. McConnell-Ginet, "The Sexual (Re)Production of Meaning," 43.
4. Scott, *The American Woman,* 5. See also Johnston, *Cherokee Women in Crisis;* Perdue, *Cherokee Women;* and Riley, *Women and Indians on the Frontier.*
5. Smith, *A Poetics of Women's Autobiography,* 125.
6. Olney, *Metaphors of Self,* v.
7. Rhoda Pitchlynn to Peter Pitchlynn, 26 October 1841.

INTRODUCTION: GENERAL HISTORY

1. La Vere, *Contrary Neighbors,* 154.
2. Morgan and Morgan, *Oklahoma,* 34.
3. Ibid., 35.
4. Ibid., 37–38.
5. Shirley, *Law West of Fort Smith,* 21.
6. Shirley, *West of Hell's Fringe,* 15–16.
7. Morgan and Morgan, *Oklahoma,* 62. See also Hale, "European Immigrants in Oklahoma," 179–203.
8. McReynolds, *Oklahoma: A History of the Sooner State,* 279.
9. Morgan and Morgan, *Oklahoma,* 55.
10. Ibid., 59.
11. For a detailed treatment of the forces agitating for the opening of Indian lands, see Gittinger, *Formation of the State of Oklahoma.*

203

12. Champagne, *Chronology of Native North American History,* 239.
13. Debo, *And Still the Waters Run,* chap. 4.
14. Morgan and Morgan, *Oklahoma,* 53.

CHAPTER 1 INTRODUCTION

1. Writers' Program of the Work Projects Administration, *Oklahoma: A Guide to the Sooner State,* 51.
2. Morgan and Morgan, *Oklahoma,* 38–39.

CHAPTER 1 INTERVIEWS

1. Indian Territory was created by the United States government in the early 1800s as an area to place Indians from the eastern part of the country. Originally, its boundaries were the Arkansas and Missouri borders on the east, the Great Bend of the Missouri River in Nebraska on the north, the Red River on the south, and the 100th meridian on the west. During the 1830s, it became home to the Cherokees, Choctaws, Creeks, Chickasaws, and Seminoles and other Indians removed from the East over the Trail of Tears. By the 1850s, the borders of Indian Territory had shrunk to roughly what is present-day Oklahoma. After the Civil War, the western part of the territory became home to reservations for the indigenous peoples of the Southern Plains such as the Comanches, Kiowas, Cheyennes, Wichitas, and Caddos. Waldman, *Atlas of the North American Indian,* 181–83.
2. Greer County was the southwestern-most tip of Indian Territory, west of the North Fork of the Red River. For years, Texas and Indian Territory argued over who owned this part of the Southern Plains. In 1896, the Supreme Court ruled that Greer County belonged to the newly created Oklahoma Territory. Morris, Goins, and McReynolds, *Historical Atlas,* map 48.
3. In 1890, the United States government split Indian Territory in two. The eastern half, where the Choctaws, Cherokees, Creeks, Chickasaws, Seminoles, and other eastern Indians lived, continued to be called "Indian Territory." The western half of the territory, where the Comanches, Kiowas, Caddos, Wichitas, Cheyennes, Arapahos, and other Southern Plains peoples lived, became Oklahoma Territory. In 1907 they would be joined to form the State of Oklahoma. Morris, Goins, and McReynolds, *Historical Atlas,* map 55.
4. During cattle drives from the 1860s through the 1880s, Splenic Fever, or anthrax, often came with tick-infested cattle coming up the trails from Texas. Ranchers in Indian Territory and Kansas feared their own cattle being contaminated by these animals with highly contagious and lethal disease.
5. Dugouts were homes burrowed out of riverbanks or hills, used by many early settlers before they could import wood or brick for houses. Dugouts functioned almost as underground houses, normally cool in the

summer and warm in the winter. But, as later interviews attest, they were plagued with dust, dirt, vermin, and snakes.

6. "Gyppy water" was water with a high mineral content, often tasting too salty or bitter, burning the mouth, and purging a person's bowels.

7. Quanah Parker was one of the greatest of the Comanche chiefs. His father was Comanche Chief Peta Nocona, while his mother was famous Texas captive Cynthia Ann Parker. As a tribal leader, Quanah fought the United States in the 1874–1875 Red River War and was one of the last Comanches to surrender to U.S. forces. After this, Quanah became a strong Progressive who advocated close ties with the United States. During the late nineteenth and early twentieth centuries, as spokesman for the Comanches he was the person with whom United States officials and reservation officers dealt. Quanah strongly supported leasing out Comanche reservation land to Texas cattle companies in the 1880s, and in gratitude some of the companies built him a large, two-story house, complete with huge stars painted on it near Cache, Oklahoma. Here Quanah and his five wives lived until his death February 25, 1911. Hagan, *Quanah Parker.*

8. Fort Sill, originally called Camp Washita, was built by Major General Philip H. Sheridan in 1869 near present-day Lawton, Oklahoma, in the southwest part of Indian Territory. It was named after Sheridan's West Point classmate Brigadier General Joshua W. Sill, who was killed in the Civil War. The first post commander was Brevet General Benjamin Grierson. Fort Sill became, and still remains, a major army post on the Southern Plains. Built to fight the Comanches, Kiowas, and other Southern Plains Indians, it sometimes served as a jail for Indian prisoners and captives, while its graveyard contains the remains of many Indians, including Geronimo. See Hagan, *United States–Comanche Relations*; "The History of Old Fort Sill."

9. As holding tribal lands in common became seen as a practice of the past, missionaries, friends of the Indians, and government officials called for each Indian or Indian family to receive an allotted amount of land to be used as a small farm. In 1887, Congress passed the Dawes General Allotment Act, which directed government negotiators to meet with Indian nations, to negotiate a purchase price per acre, then to break up the reservation lands and distribute them to individual Indians or heads of households. Depending on the size of the reservation, the apportionments often averaged about 160 acres, though some nations got more and others got less. Once the assignments were made, the surplus land was then sold to white settlers. For the Kiowas, Comanches, and Apaches living on the KCA Reservation in western Indian Territory, their turn came in 1892, when the Jerome Commission essentially purchased the reservation for about $2 million. For the next nine years, the government allotted 160-acre tracts to Kiowa, Comanche, and Apache residents, then in 1901 opened what was left of the now-defunct KCA Reservation to white settlers by holding a lottery. Hagan, *United States–Comanche Relations*, 251–85; La Vere, *Contrary Neighbors*, 220–22.

10. After the Dawes General Allotment Act of 1887 began breaking up and distributing reservation lands, members of Indian nations had to enroll on a census in order to receive their allotments.

11. Agencies were the headquarters of any given Indian reservation. Here the government-appointed agent lived, as did most other government employees involved in running the reservation. In this instance, Anadarko, about fifteen miles west of Chickasha, served as the agency for the Kiowas, Comanches, Wichitas, and Caddos in the area. Hagan, *United States–Comanche Relations*, 140.

12. This Supreme Court decision *(United States v. Texas)* is the 1896 ruling that gave Greer County to Oklahoma Territory rather than to Texas. See note 2 above.

13. After the reservations were broken up and the Indians received their individual land allotments, many Indians leased out their land to white workers and settlers rather than farming it themselves.

14. This was the famous 1889 Oklahoma Land Rush. At noon on April 22, 1889, a whistle was blown, and Unassigned Territory, around present-day Oklahoma City, was thrown open to settlement. Thousands of people raced into central Oklahoma, claiming homestead sites. Several other land rushes took place over the next few years. The Cheyenne-Arapaho Reservation was opened by a run on April 19, 1892, while the Cherokee Strip was opened by a run on September 16, 1893. Morris, Goins, and McReynolds, *Historical Atlas,* map 48.

15. In the 1835 Treaty of New Echota, the Cherokees essentially exchanged all their lands in the Southeast for lands in northeastern Indian Territory. In order to prevent the Cherokees from being hemmed in and unable to travel west to the Great Plains, the treaty also stipulated that an outlet would be created for them. The Cherokee Outlet, a 57-mile-wide piece of land that ran 226 miles from the northwestern boundary of the Cherokee Nation at the 96th meridian west to the 100th meridian, served this purpose. The Outlet was opened to American settlement on September 16, 1893. Morris, Goins, and McReynolds, *Historical Atlas,* map 23.

16. During the early 1860s, Jesse Chisholm was a Cherokee-Scot trader to such Central and Southern Plains Indians as the Comanches, Kiowas, Wichitas, and Caddos. In many ways, Chisholm's wagon and pack trains blazed trails across Texas and Indian Territory. In 1867, on one of the earliest Texas cattle drives to Kansas, cattleman O. W. Wheeler was moving 2,500 head of cattle north when at the North Canadian River in Indian Territory he spotted Chisholm's wagon tracks heading toward Wichita. And so began the Chisholm Trail, a major cattle artery from the Rio Grande to central Kansas. It remained so until the trail drives died in the mid-1880s. Worcester, "Chisholm Trail."

17. "Cherokee Strip" is probably a reference to the Cherokee Outlet, as the phrases were often used synonymously. See note 15 above.

18. In 1879, cattlemen driving herds into the Cherokee Outlet increased in numbers, and the Cherokee Council decided to collect money from the owners. A loose organization of cattlemen was organized to settle

disputes and to protect herds. Every member of the organization recorded his cattle brand to protect his cattle claim during the big roundups. The person mentioned probably worked for one of these "Cattle Commission companies." Milam, "The Opening," 269–71.

CHAPTER 2 INTRODUCTION

1. Writers' Program of the Work Projects Administration, *Oklahoma: A Guide to the Sooner State*, 94.
2. Wright, Shirk, and Franks, *Mark of Heritage*, 111.
3. Writers' Program of the Work Projects Administration, *Oklahoma: A Guide to the Sooner State*, 94.
4. "Oklahoma's First Telephone," 887–88.

CHAPTER 2 INTERVIEWS

1. "A major problem Indians on reservations constantly complained about was that nearby white settlers often trespassed onto the reservation and illegally cut wood and timber claimed by the Indians." La Vere, *Life among the Texas Indians*, 188, 197–98.
2. Komalty ("Komalta") was a renowned Kiowa chief who argued against the breakup and allotment of the KCA Reservation in the late nineteenth and early twentieth centuries.
3. "Many of the treaties the United States negotiated with the Indians of Oklahoma required the government to provide beef to the Indians, particularly to those Indians who would not be able to hunt buffalo once settled on the reservation. Periodically, herds of cattle would be delivered to the reservations where they would be parceled out to families and then butchered. Since Indians from all over the reservation gathered to receive their meat, Beef Issue day often took on a carnival-like atmosphere." Hagan, *United States–Comanche Relations*, 185–86.
4. Pashofa is a hominy corn and pork stew, a staple of Southeastern Indian peoples such as the Chickasaws and Choctaws.
5. The Pashofa Dance was a Choctaw dance used to cure the ill. While a medicine man attended a patient, neighbors gathered outside the house and danced, often mimicking the groans and movements of the sick person inside. After the dance, pashofa was served to all involved. Crossett, "A Vanishing Race," 100–115.
6. The Choctaws, Cherokees, Creeks, Chickasaws, and Seminoles earned the moniker "Five Civilized Tribes" because in the early 1800s they adopted habits of American civilization such as speaking English, practicing Christianity, and engaging in trade and commerce. As a result, many of these progressive Indians participated in the Southern cotton economy and owned black slaves. In fact, hundreds of slaves went over the Trail of Tears with the tribes to Oklahoma. After the Civil War, the United States government forced these Indian nations to sign the Treaty of 1866, which, among other things, compelled the tribes to give citizenship to their

former slaves. McLoughlin, *After the Trail of Tears,* 226; Perdue, "*Mixed Blood" Indians,* 65–66.

7. A section of land was one square mile or 640 acres. A quarter section was 160 acres.

8. During the 1870s, buffalo hunters almost slaughtered the American bison to extinction. Millions of buffalo were killed for their tongues, which were considered a delicacy, and for their hides, while their skinned carcasses were left dotting the Great Plains. Later, enterprising settlers gathered tons of buffalo bones and sold them to fertilizer companies.

9. In 1895, Rev. Elton Deyo and his wife, Anna, serving with the American Baptist Home Mission Society, opened a mission among the Comanches about fifteen miles southwest of Fort Sill. The gospel was preached to Fort Sill–area Indians and settlers at the Deyo Mission until Deyo's death in 1926. Jeter, "Pioneer Preacher," 358–68.

CHAPTER 4 INTRODUCTION

1. Johnston, *Cherokee Women in Crisis,* 104.
2. Morgan and Morgan, *Oklahoma,* 55.

CHAPTER 4 INTERVIEWS

1. "Wilson War" on Clear Creek likely refers to a minor battle between American Indians (probably Choctaws) and whites at the water mill on Clear Creek near Doaksville in southeastern Indian Territory rather than to the Civil War Battle of Wilson's Creek in Missouri.

2. This is a reference to one of the land runs discussed in note 14, chapter 1.

3. Buffalo chips were dried buffalo dung, which were used as fuel by people on the tree-barren Great Plains.

4. "Cwt" means hundredweight.

5. "$5.00 permit" refers to a permit needed by non-Indians to work in Indian Territory. The cost of a permit seemed to vary over time and from place to place.

6. Born in New Hampshire in 1786, Cyrus Kingsbury became a renowned Presbyterian missionary among the Choctaws, establishing a mission among them in 1818 in the Southeast. Once the tribe was removed to Indian Territory, Kingsbury followed and in 1836 established another mission at Pine Ridge, near Fort Towson. He remained among the Choctaws in Indian Territory until he died on June 27, 1870. "Cyrus Kingsbury."

7. In accordance with the 1887 Dawes Act, the Indians received land allotments, but because there were so many Cherokees and not much land in their nation, Cherokee citizens received only about eighty acres.

8. As part of the government's effort to civilize Indians and to assimilate them into mainstream American society, in 1898 Congress passed the Curtis Act, which essentially dissolved the tribal governments

of the Cherokees, Choctaws, Creeks, Chickasaws, and Seminoles. La Vere, *Contrary Neighbors*, 220.

CHAPTER 5 INTRODUCTION

1. La Vere, *Contrary Neighbors*, 7.
2. Debo, *A History of the Indians of the United States*, 168.
3. Shirley, *West of Hell's Fringe*, 16.
4. Morgan and Morgan, *Oklahoma*, 54–55.

CHAPTER 5 INTERVIEWS

1. Born in Missouri, Cole Younger was a famous outlaw in Indian Territory, who, along with the James brothers, rode with William C. Quantrill, a guerilla chieftain, during the Civil War. After the war, Cole rode with the James Gang and became the lover of Belle Starr and fathered a daughter with her. With the James brothers, Cole and his brothers Bob and Jim robbed a bank in Northfield, Minnesota, were arrested in the aftermath, and served prison terms. Harrington, *Hanging Judge*, 18, 82.

2. Myra Maybelle Shirly, better known as Belle Starr, was born in Missouri and became a well-known figure as a frontier outlaw in Indian Territory. She was one of Cole Younger's mistresses and claimed him as the father of her child. She was associated with the Felix Griffin Gang, her name was linked with the bandit Jim Reid, and she later lived with Cherokee Sam Starr, whose name she took. She was convicted of horse stealing in 1883 and served a prison term. Starr died in 1889 after being shot in the back near her home in Indian Territory. Harrington, *Hanging Judge*, 25, 37, 81, 97.

3. During the Civil War, the Indians of Indian Territory were as divided as the rest of the nation. Among the Cherokees, some supported the Confederacy and others the Union. Pins, identified by pins tucked under their collars, were Unionists and they often battled Cherokee Confederates.

4. The Dalton Gang was an outlaw gang of the early 1890s. The gang included the brothers Grat, Bob, and Emmett, who were once officers for Judge Parker's federal court in Fort Smith, Arkansas, but later became outlaws, stealing horses and robbing trains and banks. They rode through Indian Territory and often hid there. Their last robbery took place in Coffeyville, Kansas, in broad daylight. Bob and Grat were killed during a running gun battle with Coffeyville citizens, and Emmet Dalton was captured, tried, and given life imprisonment. Harrington, *Hanging Judge*, 79, 88.

5. Thomas M. Buffington was a Cherokee Nation senator and later mayor of Vinita, Oklahoma, during the 1890s. He was elected Principal Chief of the Cherokees in 1899. As Principal Chief, he oversaw the breakup and allotment of the Cherokee Nation's lands. Voted out of

office in 1903, he returned to Vinita and served as mayor for several more years. He died there on February 11, 1938. Meserve, "Chief Thomas Mitchell Buffington," 135–46.

CHAPTER 6 INTRODUCTION

1. Flickinger, *The Choctaw Freedmen*, 16–17.
2. Ibid., 101.
3. Champagne, *Chronology of Native North American History*, 224–25.
4. Wright, Shirk, and Franks, *Mark of Heritage*, 40.

CHAPTER 6 INTERVIEWS

1. Reverend T. F. Brewer probably refers to Rev. Theodore F. Brewer Born in Tennessee in 1845, Brewer served in the Confederate Army and after the war became a minister of the Methodist Episcopal Church. In 1878, the Church transferred him to Indian Territory, where he became an educator, serving as head of Asbury Manual Labor School near Eufala. He later founded the Harrell International Institute and ran it for twenty-five years before assuming presidency of Willie Halsell College in Vinita. Brewer died on April 6, 1928. The Harrell International Institute, a Methodist girl's school in Muskogee, later became the Spaulding Institute. Boys under twelve were allowed to attend; Will Rogers attended school there as a young boy. Foreman, "Mrs. Laura E. Harsha," 182; and "Necrology: Theodore F. Brewer," 232–33.
2. The Cherokee Female Seminary at Tahlequah was a girl's school opened in 1851. Modeled on Mount Holyoke College in Massachusetts, it was designed to teach Cherokee women to become teachers. Women took classes in French, Latin, trigonometry, literary criticism, and even political economy. It was not until 1905 that the curriculum shifted to teaching more of the domestic sciences. Part of the old seminary can still be seen at Northeastern State University at Tahlequah. McLoughlin, *After the Trail of Tears*, 92.
3. Chief Motey Tiger served as Creek Chief during the difficult years 1907–1917.
4. The "Boarding School for Creek Girls" at Muskogee was the Harrell's International Institute. See note 1 above.
5. The Fort Sill Indian School was a reservation school for Comanche boys and girls that opened around 1892. The Carlisle Indian School at Carlisle, Pennsylvania, was one of the first off-reservation Indian boarding schools and was probably the most famous. Opened in 1879, it drew children from Indian nations across the United States. Its students received a heavy dose of American civilization. Their hair was cut, Indian clothing was burned, speaking native languages was forbidden, and there was an emphasis on farming and carpentry for boys and sewing, cooking, and domestic work for girls. Jim Thorpe, a Sac and Fox

Indian who went on to become an Olympic track and field champion and one of the first players in the National Football League, attended Carlisle. Hagan, *United States–Comanche Relations*, 162–63, 199–200.

6. The Chilocco Indian Industrial School was an off-reservation boarding school in Kay County, Indian Territory, near the Kansas border. It opened in June 1884 and drew students from virtually every Indian nation in Indian Territory. Lomawaima, *They Called It Prairie Light.*

7. This is probably Father Isadore Ricklin, a Catholic missionary who founded St. Patrick's Mission and Boarding School in Anadarko in 1892 and served as its superintendent. Mitchell, "The Early Days of Anadarko," 392.

8. Rev. Silas V. Fait and his wife, Anna, served as Presbyterian missionaries in Anadarko. They built their mission and Presbyterian Church in 1892 to minister to the Comanches and Kiowas. They also established the Mary Gregory Memorial School a few miles east of Anadarko. Fait, "An Autobiography," 185–95.

9. Located in Lawrence, Kansas, Haskell Institute opened in 1884 as an off-reservation American Indian boarding school. Students from Indian nations across the United States were sent to Haskell to learn such jobs as tailoring, wagon making, and harness making if they were boys. Girls learned cooking, sewing, and laundering. Later, it created a normal school to train teachers. Today, Haskell offers a university curriculum and is known as Haskell Indian Nations University. Haskell Indian Nations University, "School History."

10. William Penn Adair was a Cherokee born in Georgia on April 15, 1830. His father, George Washington Adair, was one of the signers of the controversial 1835 Treaty of New Echota. Once in Indian Territory, Adair was educated at various Cherokee schools and served as a Cherokee senator from 1853 to 1860. During the Civil War, he fought for the Confederacy as a member of Cherokee general Stand Watie's Cherokee Mounted Rifles, where he rose to the rank of colonel. After the Civil War, Adair represented his tribe in Washington, D.C., He became Assistant Principal Chief of the Cherokees in 1879 and died at Tahlequah on October 23, 1882. "Adair County, Oklahoma."

11. Lillian Nordica became a famous American opera soprano during the late nineteenth and early twentieth centuries. Born in 1856 in Farmington, Maine, she became internationally known, especially for portraying Wagnerian heroines. Madame Nordica died on May 10, 1914, on the island of Java while on a worldwide tour. Suhm-Binder, "Nordica, Lillian."

12. Known as "the Divine Sarah," Sarah Bernhardt was born in Paris on October 22, 1844, and died there in 1923. Bernhardt was one of the most celebrated actresses of her time and toured internationally. *Encyclopaedia Britannica*, "Bernhardt, Sarah."

13. Madame Ernestine Schumann-Heink was born near Prague in 1861 and became one of the great internationally known opera singers of the late nineteenth and early twentieth centuries. Considered the greatest

contralto of her time, she died on November 17, 1936, in Hollywood, California. Amero, "The Magic of Madame Schumann-Heink."

14. The Stomp Dance is a ceremonial circling dance led by a male followed by a female shell shaker wearing on her legs rattles formed from terrapin shells or small cans filled with pebbles. This is a Southeastern dance performed by Cherokees, Natchez-Cherokees, Creeks, Seminoles, Yuchis, Caddos, Shawnees, Choctaws, and Chickasaws. See Hudson, *The Southeastern Indians*, 473–77.

15. Pleasant Porter served as Principal Chief of the Creek Nation from 1899 until his death in 1907. Born in 1840, he received a common-school education upon which he continued his learning, evident in his knowledge of the classics. During the Civil War, he fought for the Confederacy and in 1872 represented the Creeks in Washington, where he became well known and numbered among his friends such personages as Presidents McKinley and Theodore Roosevelt. He was known for his graciousness, his education, and his entertaining conversation. Meserve, "Chief Pleasant Porter," 318–34.

CHAPTER 7 INTRODUCTION

1. Reese, *Women of Oklahoma*, 274.
2. Ibid., 183.

Bibliography

PRIMARY SOURCES

Indian Pioneer Papers, Special Collections Division, John Vaughan Library, Northeastern State University, Tahlequah, Okla.
Pitchlynn, Rhoda, to Peter Pitchlynn, 26 October 1841, Peter Pitchlynn Collection, Box 1, Folder 70, Western History Collection, University of Oklahoma Library.

SECONDARY SOURCES

Baker, T. Lindsay, and Julie P. Baker, eds. *The WPA Oklahoma Slave Narratives*. Norman: University of Oklahoma Press, 1996.
Bataille, Gretchen M., and Kathleen M. Sands. *American Indian Women: Telling Their Lives*. Lincoln: University of Nebraska Press, 1984.
Champagne, Duane, ed. *Chronology of Native North American History: From Pre-Columbian Times to the Present*. Detroit: Gale Research, 1994.
Crossett, G. A. "A Vanishing Race." *Chronicles of Oklahoma* 4, no. 2 (1926): 100–115.
Debo, Angie. *A History of the Indians of the United States*. Norman: University of Oklahoma Press, 1970.
———. *And Still the Waters Run: The Betrayal of the Five Civilized Tribes*. 1940. Reprint, Norman: University of Oklahoma Press, 1989.
Encyclopaedia Britannica, 15th ed., Micropaedia, s.v. "Bernhardt, Sarah."
Fait, Anna R. "An Autobiography." *Chronicles of Oklahoma* 32, no. 2 (1954): 185–95.
Flickinger, Robert Elliott. *The Choctaw Freedmen and the Story of Oak Hill Industrial Academy*. Pittsburgh, Pa.: Presbyterian Board of Missions for Freedmen, 1914.

Foreman, Carolyn Thomas. "Mrs. Laura E. Harsha." *Chronicles of Oklahoma* 18, no. 2 (1940): 182.

Foreman, Grant. *Down the Texas Road: Historic Places along Highway 69 through Oklahoma.* Norman: University of Oklahoma Press, 1936.

———. *Indian Removal: The Emigration of the Five Civilized Tribes of Indians.* Norman: University of Oklahoma Press, 1932.

Foreman, Grant, and Carolyn Thomas Foreman. *Fort Gibson: A Brief History.* Muskogee, Okla.: Hoffman-Speed Printing, 1970.

Gittinger, Roy. *Formation of the State of Oklahoma, 1803–1906.* Norman: University of Oklahoma Press, 1939.

Hagan, William T. *Quanah Parker, Comanche Chief.* Norman: University of Oklahoma Press, 1993.

———. *United States–Comanche Relations: The Reservation Years.* Norman: University of Oklahoma Press, 1976.

Hale, Douglas. "European Immigrants in Oklahoma: A Survey." *Chronicles of Oklahoma* 53, no. 2 (1975): 179–203.

Harrington, Fred Harvey. *Hanging Judge.* Caldwell, Idaho: Caxton Printers, 1951.

Hopkins, Sarah Winnemucca. *Life among the Piutes: Their Wrongs and Claims.* Reno: University of Nevada Press, 1994.

Hudson, Charles M. *The Southeastern Indians.* Knoxville: University of Tennessee Press, 1976.

Jeter, Jerry B. "Pioneer Preacher." *Chronicles of Oklahoma* 23, no. 4 (Winter 1945–46): 358–68.

Johnston, Carolyn Ross. *Cherokee Women in Crisis: Trail of Tears, Civil War, and Allotment, 1838–1907.* Tuscaloosa: University of Alabama Press, 2003.

La Vere, David. *Contrary Neighbors: Southern Plains and Removed Indians in Indian Territory.* Norman: University of Oklahoma Press, 2000.

———. *Life among the Texas Indians: The WPA Narratives.* College Station: Texas A&M University Press, 1998.

Linderman, Frank B. *Pretty-Shield: Medicine Woman of the Crows.* 1932. Reprint, Lincoln: University of Nebraska Press, 2003.

Lomawaima, K. Tsianina. *They Called It Prairie Light: The Story of the Chilocco Indian School.* Lincoln: University of Nebraska Press, 1994.

McConnell-Ginet, Sally. "The Sexual (Re)Production of Meaning: A Discourse-Based Theory." In *Language, Gender, and Professional Writing: Theoretical Approaches and Guidelines for Nonsexist Usage,* edited by Francine Wattman Frank and Paula A. Treichler. New York: Modern Language Association of America, 1989. 35–50.

McLoughlin, William G. *After the Trail of Tears: The Cherokees' Struggle for Sovereignty, 1839–1880.* Chapel Hill: University of North Carolina Press, 1993.

McReynolds, Edwin C. *Oklahoma: A History of the Sooner State.* Norman: University of Oklahoma Press, 1954.

Meserve, John Bartlett. "Chief Pleasant Porter." *Chronicles of Oklahoma* 9, no. 3 (1931): 318–34.

———. "Chief Thomas Mitchell Buffington and Chief William Charles Rogers." *Chronicles of Oklahoma* 17, no. 2 (1939): 135–46.

Milam, Joe B. "The Opening of the Cherokee Outlet." *Chronicles of Oklahoma* 9, no. 3 (1931): 269–71.

Mitchell, Sara Brown. "The Early Days of Anadarko." *Chronicles of Oklahoma* 28, no. 4 (1950): 392.

Morgan, H. Wayne, and Anne Hodges Morgan. *Oklahoma: A History.* New York: Norton, 1984.

Morris, John W., Charles R. Goins, and Edwin C. McReynolds. *Historical Atlas of Oklahoma,* 3rd ed. Norman: University of Oklahoma Press, 1986.

"Necrology: Theodore F. Brewer." *Chronicles of Oklahoma* 6, no. 2 (1928): 232–33.

"Oklahoma's First Telephone." *Chronicles of Oklahoma* 11, no. 3 (1933): 887–88.

Olney, James. *Metaphors of Self: The Meaning of Autobiography.* Princeton: Princeton University Press, 1972.

Perdue, Theda. *Cherokee Women: Gender and Culture Change, 1700–1835.* Lincoln: University of Nebraska Press, 1998.

———. *"Mixed Blood" Indians: Racial Construction in the Early South.* Athens: University of Georgia Press, 2003.

———. *Nations Remembered: An Oral History of the Cherokees, Chickasaws, Choctaws, Creeks, and Seminoles in Oklahoma, 1865–1907.* Norman: University of Oklahoma Press, 1993.

Rebolledo, Tey Diana, and María Teresa Márquez, eds. *Women's Tales from the New Mexico WPA: La Diabla a Pie.* Houston: Arte Público Press, 2000.

Reese, Linda Williams. *Women of Oklahoma, 1890–1920.* Norman: University of Oklahoma Press, 1997.

Riley, Glenda. *Women and Indians on the Frontier, 1825–1915.* Albuquerque: University of New Mexico Press, 1984.

Scott, Anne Firor. *The American Woman: Who Was She?* Englewood Cliffs, N.J.: Prentice-Hall, 1971.

Shirley, Glenn. *Law West of Fort Smith: A History of Frontier Justice in the Indian Territory, 1834–1896.* Lincoln: University of Nebraska Press, 1968.

———. *West of Hell's Fringe: Crime, Criminals, and the Federal Peace Officer in Oklahoma Territory, 1889–1907.* Norman: University of Oklahoma Press, 1978.

Smith, Sidonie. *A Poetics of Women's Autobiography: Marginality and the Fictions of Self-Representation.* Bloomington: Indiana University Press, 1987.

Waldman, Carl. *Atlas of the North American Indian.* New York: Facts on File, 1985.

Wright, J. Leitch, Jr. *The Only Land The Knew: The Tragic Story of the American Indians in the Old South.* New York: Free Press, 1981.

Wright, Muriel H., George H. Shirk, and Kenny A. Franks. *Mark of Heritage*. Oklahoma City: Oklahoma Historical Society, 1976.

Writers' Program of the Work Projects Administration in the State of Oklahoma. *Oklahoma: A Guide to the Sooner State*. Norman: University of Oklahoma Press, 1941.

ELECTRONIC SOURCES

"Adair County, Oklahoma." Leisure and Sport Review. http://www.lasr .net/leisure/oklahoma/adair/.

Amero, Richard W. "The Magic of Madame Schumann-Heink." http:// members.cox.net/ramero/scheink.htm.

"Cyrus Kingsbury." Virtualology Web site. http://www.famousamericans .net/cyruskingsbury/.

Haskell Indian Nations University. "School History." Haskell Indian Nations University. http://www.haskell.edu/haskell/about.asp.

"The History of Old Fort Sill." Fort Sill Web site. http://sill-www.army .mil/pao/pahist.htm.

Suhm-Binder, Andrea. "Nordica, Lillian." Cantabile-Subito Web site. http:// www.cantabile-subito.de/Sopranos/Nordica__Lillian/nordica__ lillian.htm.

Worcester, Donald E. "Chisholm Trail." Handbook of Texas History Online. http://www.tsha.utexas.edu/handbook/online/articles/CC/ ayc2.html.

Index